MITHRAS-ORION

ÉTUDES PRÉLIMINAIRES
AUX RELIGIONS ORIENTALES
DANS L'EMPIRE ROMAIN

PUBLIÉES PAR

M. J. VERMASEREN

TOME QUATRE-VINGT ET UNIÈME

MICHAEL P. SPEIDEL

MITHRAS - ORION

LEIDEN
E. J. BRILL
1980

Cult Icon of the Mithraic Temple at Heddernheim Germany. Museum Wiesbaden.

Museum Photograph, Neg. N2. A 1/65/2

MICHAEL P. SPEIDEL

MITHRAS–ORION

GREEK HERO AND ROMAN ARMY GOD

WITH A FRONTISPIECE, 1 PLATE AND 8 FIGURES

LEIDEN
E. J. BRILL
1980

ISBN 90 04 06055 3

PRINTED IN BELGIUM

To

GISELA

Remembering Athens, Ephesus, Byzantion,
Amida, Edessa, Arsameia, Satala, Samosata, Zeugma,
Nisibis, Ecbatana, Persepolis, Palmyra, and the many other places
of our Herodotan researches

CONTENTS

FOREWORD

Of the new religions that swept across the Roman empire as forerunners of Christianity, Mithraism, together with the cult of Iuppiter Dolichenus, was the most successful in the Roman army. Ostensibly an Iranian cult, it actually was a Greek cosmic religion, based on the Greek view of the heavens and the myth of Orion. This, at any rate, is the thesis of the present essay. If true, it will define in a new way an essential element in the spiritual life of the Roman army and the Roman empire.

The thesis proffered here rests on the observation that the elements of the Mithraic cult icon represent, on one level, a coherent series of equatorial constellations. If so, Mithras there takes the place of Orion, and one may ask how much of the myth of Orion underlies the myth of Mithras. The present study is limited in scope to this observation and this question: it does not purport to describe the many other aspects of Roman Mithraism.

To the University of Hawaii I owe a debt of gratitude for its fine working conditions and its stimulating community of scholars. From the other side of the globe, the Syrian National Museum at Damascus has generously supplied photographs, drawings, offprints, and detailed information in a way few museums in the world could excel. The American National Endowment for the Humanities enabled me to visit the archaeological sites and museums of West Asia and thus to discover the remarkable bronze at Damascus (plate I).

Four friends greatly contributed to this study: Professor James D. Lind did the line drawings; Professor John J. Stephan improved upon the phraseology; Dr. Hannsjörg Ubl of the Austrian *Bundesdenkmalamt* gave of his splendid knowledge of Roman monuments in spirited discussions in the Hauran mountains of Syria and along Trajan's road down to the Red Sea; Professor Maarten J. Vermaseren courageously included the essay in his series of preliminary studies on the Oriental religions in the Roman empire.

University of Hawaii at Manoa   Spring 1979
Honolulu

1. INTRODUCTION

> Different people worshipped Mithras differently, some as the Sun god, others as the guardian of the fire, still others as a specific power. And there arose a certain mystery religion of Mithras, especially among astrologers.
>
> Nonnos Mythographos [1]

Mithras is mankind's oldest living god. The record of his cult goes farther back through the millennia than that of any other god still worshipped. The Aryan Mitanni of Upper Mesopotamia, in a treaty with the neighbouring Hittites, invoke him in the fourteenth century B.C. as one of the guarantors of the treaty. India's sacred literature refers to him since the hymns of the Rig Veda. But it was in Iran where Mithras rose to the greatest prominence: rebounding after the reforms of Zarathustra, Mithras became one of the great gods of the Achaemenian emperors and to this very day he is worshipped in India and Iran by Parsees and Zarathustrians.

Roman Mithraism has a history apart. As a mystery religion it engulfed the Roman empire during the first four centuries of our era. Mithraic sanctuaries are found from Roman Arabia to Britain, from the Danube to the Sahara, wherever the Roman soldier went. Christian apologetics fiercely fought the cult they feared, and during the late fourth century A.D., as a victim of the Judaeo-Christian spirit of intolerance, Roman Mithraism was suppressed, its sanctuaries destroyed together with the last vestiges of religious freedom in the empire.

---

[1] F. Cumont (1896 : 28): Τὸν Μίθραν ἄλλοι ἄλλως ἐνόμισαν· οἱ μὲν γὰρ τὸν ἥλιον, οἱ δὲ τὸν ἔφορον τοῦ πυρός, ἄλλοι δὲ εἰδικήν τινα δύναμιν. γίνονται δὲ τούτῳ τῷ Μίθρᾳ τινὲς τελεταὶ καὶ μάλιστα παρὰ Χαλδαίοις. The information value of this text is much depreciated by F. Cumont (1899: 30) but Nonnos' further information on ordeals in the cult has been substantiated to some extent by finds made since, see e.g. M. J. Vermaseren and C. C. van Essen (1965: 144) and M. J. Vermaseren (1971: 43 ff.). This essay was researched with the help of a grant from the National Endowment for the Humanities, Research Materials Division. The views presented here are not necessarily those of the Endowment. The grant made it possible to enlist the skillful and dedicated services of Ms. Lynn Maruyama 'attending all problems with speed and indefatigable vigor' (below, p. 40).

What made Western Mithraism so attractive that it could acquire such a widespread following in the Roman army? Was it Iranian dualism, the eternal fight between good and evil, between light and darkness that proved to be akin to the Roman way of unsparing self-exertion in the face of danger? There is indeed much tangible Iranian in the cult: not only is Mithras' name Iranian but so is his dress; the Iranian devil Ahriman is invoked in the cult, the Iranian holy word *nama* is used, one of the seven grades of initiation is *Persa*, and as our texts show, the Romans themselves believed Mithraism to have come from Iran. This provoked Franz Cumont, the pioneer of Mithraic studies, to exclaim that: 'Never, not even during the Mohammedan invasions, had Europe a narrower escape from becoming Asiatic than when Diocletian officially recognized Mithras as the protector of the reconstructed empire'.[2] Cumont believed that Mithraism 'always remained in substance a Mazdaism blended with Chaldeanism, that is to say, essentially a barbarian religion.... For that reason it always seemed unacceptable to the Greek world.... The Greeks never admitted the god of their hereditary enemies, and the great centers of Hellenic civilization escaped his influence and he theirs. Mithraism passed directly from Asia into the Latin world'.[3]

The opposite is true. Mithraism is originally and substantially a Greek religion with only a few Iranian elements. The detailed demonstration of this is not the subject of the essay presented here. The method followed is not to search for compatibilities or incompatibilities between Iranian and Western Mithraic tradition, a procedure that has led to a certain wantonness. Instead, an attempt is made to show by direct proof that the cosmic meaning of Mithraism is the essential and original one,—and Greek throughout.

Admittedly, the stars will prove whatever one wants them to prove. Therefore, contrary to its appearance, this study is not based on the testimony of the night sky. Quite differently, its observations are

---

[2] F. Cumont (1911:142). For Iranian elements in Roman Mithraism see now G. Widengren (1966) whose work represents the high-water mark of the belief in an essentially Iranian Mithraism. Contra: S. Wikander (1950), R.L. Gordon (1975), M.J. Vermaseren (1978: 25ff). Mitanni: CIMRM 16.

[3] F. Cumont (1911:148f.).

found in the ancient views of the sky such as they have come down to us in ancient globes, poems, and school books of astronomy. These hitherto neglected sources, when confronted with Mithraic literature, art, and inscriptions, will demonstrate that the cult icon, i.e. the bull slaying scene, represents the equatorial summer constellations. They will further show that Mithras is the constellation Orion, the resplendent 'leader under whom the constellations wheel through the whole of heaven'[4], and under whom soldiers are born. Finally, it will appear that the myth of Mithras is largely the myth of the Greek hero Orion.

---

[4] Manilius 1, 395 (= E. A. Housman, I: 40): *hoc duce per totum decurrunt sidera mundum.*

2. THE BULL SLAYING SCENE AS A SERIES OF EQUATORIAL CONSTELLATIONS

The bull slaying scene is the essential icon of Western Mithraism. Carved and painted in the cult niches of sanctuaries throughout the Roman empire, it portrays with remarkable regularity Mithras turned to the right, coming upon the bull from behind, pressing his left knee on the back of the animal. The bull is crouching, its right foreleg is sharply bent. With left hand Mithras holds the bull by the mouth, jerking the animal's head backwards, while with his right hand he thrusts a sword into the bull's shoulder. Mithras and the bull are surrounded by other figures: a dog leaps up at the bull's wound, a snake glides along the bottom, a scorpion attacks the bull's genitals, and higher up there sits a raven. Sometimes a lion squats next to

Fig. 1. Cult icon from Heddernheim/Germany. (Frontispiece)

a mixing bowl and the tail of the bull ends in ears of corn. The rising sun and the setting moon frequently surmount the scene, while the twin gods Cautes and Cautopates with their torches stand on the sides, Cautes' torch pointing up, Cautopates' torch pointing down. A rocky cave, at times with a zodiac arching over it, often serves to indicate the locale.

Over five hundred such representations of the bull slaying scene have been found, most of them with only minor variations. Hence, there can be no doubt that they express the central myth of the cult. Yet in the almost complete absence of theological or liturgical literature of Roman Mithraism, the scene and the myth it portrays, have remained only dimly understood. To unlock the secret of the icon, three fields of investigation have been combed for comparative and relevant material:

1. Iranian religious literature
2. Greek and Roman art
3. Astral and seasonal symbolism.[1]

None of these have provided a unified, compelling explanation of the scene. Therefore, and because the many astral features of the Mithraic sanctuaries point to a cosmic meaning of the icon, the answer may be found in a somewhat different field, i.e.

4. Greek and Roman astronomy.

We have it on ancient authority that the bull on which Mithras is kneeling is the constellation Taurus. Porphyry, writing in the later third century A.D. when Mithraism had reached its climax, states in his treatise 'On the Cave of the Nymphs' that Mithras carries the sword of Aries, i.e. the zodiacal sign of Mars, and that he rides 'on the bull of Venus', i.e. Taurus, the zodiacal sign of Venus.[2] Since

---

[1] For explanations of the bull slaying scene with the aid of Iranian religious concepts see e.g. F. Cumont (1899), G. Widengren (1966), and L. A. Campbell (1968). For Greek and Roman art: F. Saxl (1931) and E. Will (1955). For astral and seasonal symbolism: K. B. Stark (1868), R. Beck (1977), and S. Insler (1978); cf. R. L. Gordon (1976). For the remnants of the cult literature: M. J. Vermaseren and C. C. van Essen (1965).

[2] Porphyrius, De antro Nympharum, 24 (A. Nauck, 1886: 73): διὸ κριοῦ μὲν φέρει

the assignment of these signs as 'houses' to the planets is ubiquitous in astrology, there is not the slightest doubt that the bull of the cult relief is here identified as Taurus. A second piece of incontrovertible evidence is found on a bull slaying relief from Sidon. There the Scorpius of the Zodiac surrounding the scene doubles as the scorpion attacking the bull's genitals—, clearly, the scorpion of the cult icon is identical with the constellation Scorpius, at least in the view of this image.[3]

With the bull of the cult icon identified as Taurus and the scorpion as Scorpius, one may wonder whether the other elements of the bull slaying scene might not also represent constellations. Could one identify the raven as Corvus, the mixing bowl as Crater, the snake as Hydra, the ears of corn as Spica, the dog as Canis Minor, and finally Mithras, the sword wielding hunter of the bull as Orion? Some of these identifications have long been made, but never comprehensively, and never based on the conclusive proof that can only be found in the documented ancient views of the heavens. And among the suggestions offered, there was usually lacking the essential conclusion that Mithras is, in fact, Orion.[4] As a consequence, the underlying principle for the selection of just these constellations has remained undiscovered.

The history of the identification of the bull slaying scene with a series of constellations can be traced through three stages. In A.D. 1868 K. B. Stark suggested all the above identifications, except Mithras-Orion, describing them as summer constellations. In A.D. 1899, F. Cumont followed Stark only grudgingly. Preoccupied with Iranian mythology he declared that 'the brilliant tissue of astronomical allegories obscured the mystical meaning of the sacred images for those who had received only an imperfect initiation'. Moreover, he saw in the

---

Ἀρηίου ζῳδίου τὴν μάχαιραν, ἐποχεῖται δὲ ταύρῳ Ἀφροδίτης. For a more detailed discussion of this text see below, p. 19 ff.

[3] CIMRM 75; cf. S. Insler (1978: 523).

[4] Some aspects of Mithras as Orion are, however, described with great perception in an unpublished undergraduate thesis by R. Small, Missoula which I received by courtesy of the author in Fall 1978, after a first version of this essay had gone to the editor. S. Insler identified Mithras with Orion during the oral presentation of his paper in Teheran 1976, but the written version (1978) contains no hint of it.

constellations suggested by Stark winter constellations. Recently, S. Insler renewed Stark's identifications and by substituting Canis Minor for Canis Maior improved on their coherence. Different from Stark and in accordance with Cumont, he chose to see in them winter constellations.[5]

Such a divergence of views may militate against a stellar interpretation of the cult icon altogether. One may object that chance could play a decisive role here, and it has indeed been said that there was not an object or an animal that could not somehow be regarded as the symbol of a constellation.[6] Admittedly, the permissive methods of astrology allow all things to mean all other things—Porphyry's identification of the sword of Mithras with Aries is a case in point. Moreover, research into the symbolism of Greek and Roman cult reliefs and funerary art has produced persuasive explanations for some features of the icon that would be unwise to discard. Hence, one will accept a predominantly stellar interpretation of the entire cult icon only if solid proof is given and if stringent conditions are met. In particular, one may ask for the following three criteria:

1. All the elements of the bull slaying scene must be represented in the sky, and they must be portrayed directly, not by allusions to other objects.
2. The constellations thus found must follow a rigorous, meaningful organizing principle.
3. The celestial features invoked and their iconography must be part of the ancient views of the heaven. Hence they must be evidenced by ancient sources, not just be inferred astronomically or astrologically.

The first criterion is to make sure that elements having a namesake in the sky or some aspect in common with a celestial feature are not arbitrarily seized upon to show an astral meaning of the icon. The second criterion is to guard against the chance that even if all the elements of the scene have an identifiable counterpart somewhere among the constellations this may be due to chance rather than to a deliberate design. The third criterion, finally, is to prevent casting

---

[5] K. B. Stark (1868: 19f.); F. Cumont (1899: 200ff.); S. Insler (1978). See also R. Beck (1977: 10).

[6] F. Cumont (1923: 111).

about in the nearly limitless possibilities of ancient and modern astrology,—possibilities that will fit any theory.

The first criterion is fulfilled by the series of identifications suggested above, on condition that Cautes and Cautopates do not belong to the scene proper but to its frame, like sun and moon, a proposition to be discussed below.

The second criterion, a rigorous, meaningful organizing principle has not been met so far. Stark was right in seeing that his constellations were located between the spring and the fall equinoxes, but other than that he made no effort to establish the principle of their selection. Insler claimed that with Scorpius, Hydra, Corvus, Crater, Leo, Virgo, and Canis Minor 'the complete sky visible just on and below the ecliptic was filled with a band of continuous constellations, stretching from east to west, ... all leading to Taurus'. That claim is demonstrably wrong, for there is no coherence between Taurus and the other constellations—they are separated by Orion. (See figures 2 and 3). Moreover, the organizing principle offered, 'just on and below the ecliptic' is disconcertingly vague.

The absence of Cancer and Gemini eliminates the ecliptic, hence it remains without any conceivable meaning : it is hard to see how it could contain a myth or a theology.

A look at the Greek view of the heavens such as represented by the Atlas Farnese globe of the Hellenistic period (Fig. 2) reveals the true organizing principle. The constellations of the bull slaying scene are all lying along the equator. Along that horizontal band, almost between the points where the arc of the Zodiac cuts across it, the globe shows the following images of constellations:[7]

> Scorpius-Libra
> Hydra
> Corvus
> Virgo-Spica
> Crater-Leo
> Orion
> Taurus.

---

[7] For the Atlas Farnese globe see G. Thiele (1898) with photographs from which figure 2 was made; note the fact that the globe gives the view from the outside of the sphere, while the usual view in ancient art and on modern maps is that from the inside.

Fig. 2. Equatorial Summer Constellations on the Atlas Farnese Globe.

Canis Minor, if already recognized as a separate constellation,[8] is here covered by Atlas' hand. Scorpius, in accordance with Roman views, is seen as one with Libra : a claw of the scorpion actually holds the scale.[9]

The concept of Crater and Leo as two equatorial constellations belonging together demands some explanation. Crater on the Atlas Farnese globe is clearly equatorial, but Leo treads the heavens too far north to touch that line. In time, however, the equator shifted farther to the north in this area, and today Leo is definitely an equatorial constellation as our figure 3 shows. The passage by Hipparchus, quoted below, p. 12, states that Crater is considerably south of the equator and thus shows an awareness that the line actually passed between Crater and Leo. Ptolemy reports the stav Leonis to lie 3°10' south of the ecliptic, a star now south of the equator.[10] Nevertheless, no ancient designation of Leo as an equatorial constellation has come to our attention and perhaps none is to be expected. At any rate, in the bull slaying scene proper the lion rarely appears without the mixing bowl, and the mixing bowl always together with the lion; the two are as a rule directly connected with each other, the lion either touching the mixing bowl with its paw, or sitting next to it.[11] It would seem, then, that in the bull slaying scene Crater and Leo are treated as a pair because the equator ran between them.[12]

---

[8] Aratus in the third century B.C. does not list Canis Minor as an equatorial constellation yet he has Procyon among the weather signs, *Phaenomena* 449. See below, p. 28, note 3.

[9] See e.g. the scholia to Germanicus' *Aratus* (= A. Breysig, 1867: 189, 21) : *Scorpius enim tam suum spatium corpore quam chelis occupat librae.* Cf. H.G. Gundel (1972: 473, 45ff.).

[10] *Systems* 7, 5 (= K. Manitius - O. Neugebauer, 1963: 47).

[11] CIMRM 966; 1083; 1118; 1149; 1206; 1283; 1292; 1306; 1359; 1388; 1727; 1935; 1958; 1972; 2241; the unorthodox relief 1275, however, shows the lion removed from the Crater, higher up. Incomplete, and hence doubtful as to the original arrangement : CIMRM 1014; 1128; 2063; 2237. These are all monuments from either Germany or Dacia (except the portable bronze plaque 1727 from Pannonia); perhaps, then, the Leo-Crater group is a secondary addition. For Leo and Crater belonging together see also E. Will (1955: 408).

[12] For an ancient view, looking at Crater and Leo as one, see Vitruvius 9, 5, 2 (= Granger, 1934: 242) : *iuxta cratera et leonem navis est, quae nominatur Argo.* Since the constellation Argo does not abut the lion at all, the passage can only be understood as taking Crater and Leo as one. See also Vitruvius 9, 5, 1 (= F. Granger, 1934: 240)

A modern map of the equatorial constellations (Fig. 3) shows that today one would also include Cetus, Monoceros, and Sextans in a

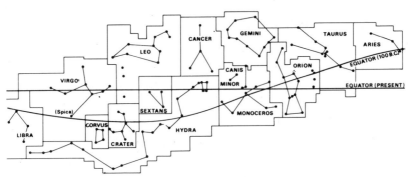

Fig. 3. The Equatorial Summer Constellations.

list of the equatorial summer constellations. Monocerus and Sextans, however, are modern creations, while Cetus is equatorial only because of the shift of the equator to the south in that area of the sky as part of the phenomenon that causes the precession of the ecliptic. For the same reasons a modern list would exclude Canis Minor, Crater, and Corvus. Yet Canis Minor is expressedly qualified as equatorial by Roman sources: Hyginus,' Latin mythographer of the second century A.D., says of it: 'it touches the equatorial circle with its feet'.[13]

Anguis (= Hydra) ... *regione Cancri erigens rostrum, ad leonem medioque corpore sustinens craterem ad manumque Virginis* (= Spica) *caudam subiciens in qua inest corvos.* In the Roman period, some five hundred years after Eudoxos, the equator had shifted enough to run decidedly north of Crater, see the passage of Hipparch or his inter-polator, quoted below, note 16. Hence it ran between Crater and Leo. Be it emphasized that this is not so much an inference from modern astronomical knowledge but from the ancient views of the sky that see Crater lying close to Leo and the equator running north of Crater. In any case Crater and Leo are rare on bull slaying scenes and probably later additions, perhaps because Leo, like the raven was an initiation grade. For Leo as a late addition see e.g. F. Saxl (1931: 65ff.); See also below, p. 29, note 4.

[13] *Astronomica* 3, 35 (= B. Bunte, Leipzig, 1875: 96) *Procyon. Hic in lacteo circulo defixus, pedibus aequinoctialem circulum tangit. Spectat ad occasum, ut inter Geminos et Cancrum constitutus.* Cf. the scholia to Germanicus' *Aratus* (A. Breysig, 1867: 182f.): *Antecanis, quem graece procyona, eo quod ante maiorem Canem exoriri videatur, appellant, est signum in lacteo circulo defixum pertingens aequinoctialem circulum, tendens ad occasum sub geminis.* See also Anonymus II, *Isagoga* 5 (= E. Maas, 1898: 114, 5).

Crater and Corvus are shown by the Atlas Farnese globe to be equatorial. What is more, by far the most influential and most widely read statement about the equator in antiquity, a passage of Aratus' *Phainomena*, written in the third century B.C. describes the equatorial constellations as follows :[14]

> Between the two tropics a circle, equal in size to the grey Milky Way, undergirts the earth as if bisecting the sphere. In it the days are equal to the nights, both at the waning of the summer and the waxing of the spring. The sign for it is the Ram and the knees of the Bull, the Ram being born lengthwise through it, but of the Bull only what is shining at the bent of the knees.
>
> In it are the belt of bright Orion and the coil of the gleaming Hydra, in it, too, the dim-lit Crater, in it Corvus and the few stars of the Scorpion's Claws. In it are born the knees of Ophiuchus, yet it has no share in the Eagle, though that mighty messenger of Zeus flies nearby. But on it wheel the head and the neck of Pegasus.

This is in full accordance with the Atlas Farnese globe and almost certainly represents Eudoxus' fourth century B.C. views.[15] However, Hipparchus in the second century B.C., or a later interpolator of his text, took into account the shift of the equator that had occurred in the meantime, criticising Aratus as follows :[16]

---

[14] Aratos, *Phainomena* 511-524 (= G. R. Mair, 1921 : 246 ff.) :

Μεσσόθι δ᾿ ἀμφοτέρων, ὅσσος πολιοῖο Γάλακτος,
γαῖαν ὑποστρέφεται κύκλος διχόωντι ἐοικώς·
ἐν δέ οἱ ἤματα νυξὶν ἰσαίεται ἀμφοτέρῃσιν,
φθίνοντος θέρεος, τοτὲ δ᾿ εἴαρος ἱσταμένοιο.
σῆμα δέ οἱ Κριὸς Ταύροιό τε γούνατα κεῖται,
Κριὸς μὲν κατὰ μῆκος ἐληλάμενος διὰ κύκλου,
Ταύρου δὲ σκελέων ὅσση περιφαίνεται ὀκλάξ.
ἐν δέ τέ οἱ ζώνη εὐφεγγέος Ὠρίωνος
καμπή τ᾿ αἰθομένης Ὕδρης· ἐνί οἱ καὶ ἐλαφρὸς
Κρητήρ, ἐν δὲ Κόραξ, ἐνὶ δ᾿ ἀστέρες οὐ μάλα πολλοὶ
Χηλάων· ἐν τῷ δ᾿ Ὀφιούχεα γοῦνα φορεῖται.
οὐ μὴν Αἰητοῦ ἀπαμείρεται, ἀλλά οἱ ἐγγὺς
Ζηνὸς ἀητεῖται μέγας ἄγγελος. ἡ δὲ κατ᾿ αὐτὸν
ἱππείη κεφαλὴ καὶ ὑπαύχενον εἰλίσσονται.

[15] Hipparch, *Commentaries* I, 1, 8 (= K. Manitius, 1894 : 6) : τῇ γὰρ Εὐδόξου συντάξει κατακολουθήσας τὰ Φαινόμενα γέγραφεν. Cf. D. R. Dicks (1970 : 151 ff.).

[16] Hipparch, *Commentaries* I, 10, 18 (= K. Manitius, 1894 : 108) : ἐν δὲ τούτοις ἠγνόηται τὰ περὶ τὸν Κριόν· ὅλος γὰρ βορειότερός ἐστι τοῦ ἰσημερινοῦ· μόνος δὲ

In this there is an error concerning Aries, for it is entirely north of the equator, only the star in its hind legs is on the equator itself.... To be sure, the belt of Orion is on the equator, but the coil of Hydra, and Crater, and Corvus are much farther south than the equator, except that the tip of the tail of Corvus touches the equator.

Whatever the truth in Hipparch's or his interpolator's statements, they were not listened to. The schoolbooks of astronomy and the many commentators and translators of Aratus perpetuated the poet's views as the popular perception—Crater and Corvus were, by and large, considered equatorial. Thus, in the second century A.D. Hyginus gives almost exactly the same description of the equator as did Aratus four hundred years earlier and he goes on to state even more positively that 'on the rear of Hydra Crater is seen with Corvus as if fixed by the equatorial circle'.[17] It follows that in both the Greek and the Roman period the constellations of the bull slaying scene were taken to be equatorial.

Aries, too, remained an equatorial constellation in the popular view, for in that sign and constellation the Zodiac crossed the equator. Aries, therefore, participated in both circles. Germanicus states in his *Aratus*

ὁ ἐν τοῖς ὀπισθίοις ποσὶν αὐτοῦ κείμενος ἀστὴρ ἐπ᾽ αὐτοῦ τοῦ ἰσημερινοῦ φέρεται. ἡ μὲν οὖν τοῦ Ὠρίωνος ζώνη κεῖται ἐπὶ τοῦ ἰσημερινοῦ· ἡ δὲ σπεῖρα τοῦ Δράκοντος καὶ ὁ Κρατὴρ καὶ ὁ Κόραξ πολλῷ νοτιώτεροί εἰσι τοῦ ἰσημερινοῦ, πλὴν εἰ ἄρα τὰ πρὸς τὴν οὐρὰν τοῦ Κόρακος συνεγγίζει τῷ ἰσημερινῷ. Very likely Hipparch's criticism here is a much later interpolation, see K. Manitius (1894: 297).

[17] Hyginus, *Astronomica* 4, 3 (= *Bunte, 1875: 102) : et ex inferiore corpore Hydrae Crater cum Corvo velut fixus esse circulo conspicitur*. See also Germanicus' *Aratus* 501-507 (= D. B. Gain, 1976: 36 f.) :
   'signa Aries Taurusque aequo tanguntur ab orbe
   sed princeps Aries totus fulgebit in illo ;
   Tauri armum subit et flexi duo sidera cruris.
   at medium Oriona secat spiramque priorem
   Hydri, tum Cratera levem Corvique forantis
   ultima, deficiunt nigra qua sidera cauda.
   illic et Chelas transverso lumine quaeres'.
Compare Hipparch's perceptive statement that the fine style of Aratus' poem gives it a certain credibility and that almost all commentators stick to his views (*Commentaries* I, 1, 7 = K. Manitius, 1894, 4ff.): ἡ γὰρ τῶν ποιημάτων χάρις ἀξιοπιστίαν τινὰ τοῖς λεγομένοις περιτίθησι, καὶ πάντες σχεδὸν οἱ τὸν ποιητὴν τοῦτον ἐξηγούμενοι προστίθενται τοῖς ὑπ᾽ αὐτοῦ λεγομένοις.

that the equator and the ecliptic are joined by a number of constellations they have in common.[18] Indeed, Aries is considered the first sign of the Zodiac[19] as well as the first sign of the equator,[20] the equator being marked by its own constellations like the Zodiac.[21] Moreover, Aries, contrary to Hipparch's opinion, is seen as right on the equator itself,—that at least is how Germanicus still puts it in the first century A.D. :[22]

> The signs of Aries and Taurus are touched by the equator
> But all of Aries shines first in it
> While Taurus reaches it with its shoulder and the two stars of the bent knee.

Aries, of course, is not depicted in the bull slaying scene, which is concerned with the constellations from Taurus to Scorpius; but since Aries was traditionally the first sign of the Zodiac and of the equator, it may have been rationalized into the picture at a later time in the tortuous way described by Porphyry in the passage quoted, i.e. the sword of Mithras was taken to refer to Mars, and Mars was taken to refer to Aries, his 'house'. Perhaps this was not only Porphyry's personal enlargement upon Mithraic theology but actually seen so by the Mithraists themselves, for a famous hexameter found on the wall of the Mithraeum at Santa Prisca in Rome reads :[23]

> Here, too, the Ram runs first, and more strictly in line.

This passage has frequently been interpreted as referring to the Zodiac,[24] but it is clearly concerned with *both* the Zodiac and the

---

[18] Germanicus, *Aratus* 501-503 quoted in the preceding note.

[19] See e.g. Manilius, *Astronomicon* I, 263 (= A. E. Housman, 1937: 26):
aurato princeps Aries in vellere fulgens.
Compare the Scholia to Germanicus' *Aratus* (A. Breysig, 1867: 80): *Nigidius hunc arietem dicit ducem et principium esse signorum.*

[20] Germanicus, *Aratus* 502 (= D. B. Gain, 1976): *sed princeps Aries totus fulgebit in illo.*

[21] Aeatus, *Phainomena*, 465, translated, e.g. by Cicero, *Aratea*, 238 (= V. Buescu, 1941: 227): *orbes stelligeri, portantes signa.*

[22] See note 17. See also the scholia in Aratus, *Prolegomena* 20 (= J. Martin, 1975: 29, 16): μέσον γὰρ τὸν Κριὸν τέμνει οὗτος ὁ κύκλος.

[23] M. J. Vermaseren - C. C. van Essen (1965: 213): *Primus et hic aries astrictius ordine currit.* For the role of the sword in a Mithraic cave see R. L. Gordon (1976).

[24] M. J. Vermaseren - C. C. van Essen (1965: 213), despite their different interpretation

equator, as is obvious from the phrase 'here, too' which presupposes that Aries is looked at in two places. The similarity of the Santa Prisca hexameter and the line of Germanicus quoted above is so great it can hardly be due to coincidence :

Primus et hic Aries astrictius ordine currit

and

Sed princeps Aries totus fulgebit in illo.

It seems safe, therefore, to assume that the Santa Prisca hexameter comes from a similar context, a description of the equator with its constellations, preceded by a description of the zodiac with its constellations in the manner of Aratus' poem.[25] The interest of the Mithraists in Aries is remarkable and may (or may not) confirm Porphyry's view that Mithras' sword means Aries. What the hexameter from Santa Prisca does bear out for certain, however, is the concern of the Mithraists with the equator.

The ears of corn in the bull slaying scene are another instance of the equatorial interest of Mithraism. Aratus already depicts Virgo with an ear of corn in her hands, while Hyginus says 'with her right hand

---

of the line do not fail to point out that *ordo* can mean a celestial course, as does rightly S. Insler (1978: 536) with a reference to Vergil, *Georgics*, 1, 238f. : *et via* (= ecliptic) *secta per ambas, obliquus qua se signorum vertet ordo* (= zodiac). Cf. R. Turcan (1975: 85), and M. J. Vermaseren (1974: 26ff.) with literature.

[25] Aratus describes first the equator, then the zodiac; but in Roman times greater stress was put on Aries being first and as a consequence even the description of the zodiac came first, see e.g. Manilius, *Astronomicon* I, 256 (= A. E. Housman, 1937: 25) :

nunc tibi signorum lucentis undique flammas
omnia quae possis caelo numerare sereno,
ordinibus certis referam. primumque canentur
quae media obliquo praecingunt ordine mundum
solemque alternis vicibus per tempora portant
atque alia adverso luctantia sidera mundo.
ut sit idem mundi primum quod continet arcem,
aurato princeps Aries in vellere fulgens
etc.

In Aries the order of the cosmos began at the beginning of time, see Housman, l.c. and the poem *on the Sphere* (Maas, 1898: 162) :

Ἄθρει δέ, κόσμου τὸν δι᾽ αἰῶνος δρόμον
ὡς εὖ διεστάθμησεν αὐτουργὸς φύσις.
Πρῶτος χορείας Κριὸς ἡγεῖται κύκλου.

she touches the equator' and 'she has single stars in each hand of which the bigger and brighter one in her right hand is called ear of corn'.[26] Similarly, the Atlas Farnese globe shows Virgo holding an ear of corn in that hand which touches the equator. (Fig. 2) One may object that the star in question, Spica, translates as 'ear of corn' in the singular, while the bull slaying scene depicts not one but three ears of corn. That discrepancy is easily reconciled, however, for there exist ancient descriptions of Spica as representing not one, but several ears of corn.[27] It is certainly remarkable that instead of the well-known constellation and zodiacal sign Virgo, one finds on the bull slaying scene only Spica, i.e. Virgo's equatorial portion.

Frequently Leo, Crater, Spica, and even Corvus[28] are missing from the cult icon; at other times they are lifted up into different positions so that only the dog, the snake, and the scorpion are found underneath Mithras and the bull. This basic version of the scene, which was perhaps the original one, still represents a continuous band of constellations along the equator from Scorpius to Taurus and thus constitutes a complete and meaningful cosmic icon.

Cautes and Cautopates might perhaps be expected to stand for the constellation Gemini. However, their position in the icon, to the side, sometimes missing or represented on side panels, and rarely ever participating in the action, suggests that the twin gods are not parts of the bull slaying scene in the same way as the dog, the snake, and the scorpion, but that like the sun, the moon, the zodiac, and the cave

---

[26] Aratus, *Phaenomena* 97: Παρθένον, ἥ ῥ' ἐν χερσὶ φέρει Στάχυν αἰγλήεντα. Hyginus, *Astronomica* 3, 24: *dextra manu circulum aequinoctialem tangit; praeterea habet in utrisque manibus singulas stellas; quarum una, quae est in dextra manu, maior et clarior. ea* στάχυς *dicitur.* (= B. Bunte, 1875:91f.). Cf. the emendation by Wilamowitz, reported by K. Robert (1878:85). Erastothenes, *Catasterismi* 9 and those who follow him see Spica in the left hand of Virgo and consequently must visualize her as turned towards the terrestrial viewer, cf. K. Robert (1878:84f.), yet Robert's emendation in Hyginus' passage, *sinistra* for *dextra* seems wrong, as there the right hand is also said to touch the equator and as Spica certainly is an equatorial star (see Ptolemy, *Systems* 7, 3 (= K. Manitius - O. Neugebauer, 1963:21 and 24ff.)—evidently Hyginus saw Virgo as turning her back on the terrestrial viewer.
[27] Teukros (TR) 6 (= F. Boll, 1903:18, cf. 129f.): οἱ στάχυες. For ancient pictures of Virgo holding three ears of corn see Boll (1903:13).
[28] E.g. CIMRM 1314.

they belong to its framework, symbolizing its cosmic setting.[29] The image of the cosmos portrayed in the bull slaying scene thus may be sketched as follows :

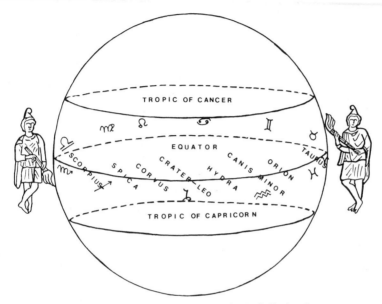

Fig. 4. The Image of the Cosmos in the Bull Slaying Scene.

The dispute whether the constellations of the bull slaying scene are summer or winter constellations is, of course, vain, for it simply depends on whether one looks at the morning sky or the evening sky. The phrase 'summer constellations', used here, is chosen in accordance with ancient usage to denote the fact that the constellations of the bull slaying scene undergirt that area of the zodiac through which the sun travels during the later spring and summer.[30]

---

[29] For Cautes and Cautopates as representing the sun on the tropics of Cancer and Capricorn see below, p. 42. For the cosmos as a rocky cave in Roman art see e.g. M. Guarducci (1959).

[30] E.g. Hyginus, *Astronomica* 4, 5 (= B. Bunte, 1875: 104) : *Aries, Taurus, Gemini, in his tribus signis ver demonstratur et aequinoctium vernum. Cancer, Leo, Virgo, in his tribus signis maxime aestas conficitur,* etc.

Why were only the constellations from Taurus to Scorpius taken into the cult icon, and not the equally equatorial Ophiuchus, Aquila Pegasus and Aries? The constellations selected for the icon are all those visible together at any one time along the equator behind Taurus and Orion, i.e. their selection is determined by what could be seen together as an icon in the sky.[31] Hence one need not search for a primarily seasonal meaning of the scene.[32]

All three criteria set up above are thus fulfilled. Firstly, all the elements of the bull slaying scene are represented together in the heavens. Secondly, the constellations thus found follow the rigid organizing principle of lying along the equator in one uninterrupted sequence from Taurus to Scorpius. Thirdly, they are all anciently attested as equatorial constellations (with the minor, and well explained exception of Leo). This in itself constitutes proof for the cosmic origin and meaning of the bull slaying scene. However, independent proof exists for the figure of Mithras-Orion himself and consequently also for the symbolism of the celestial equator.

---

[31] See e.g. Aratus, *Phaenomena*, 645f. (= G. R. Mair, 1921 : 256) :

τούνεκα δὴ καί φασι περαιόθεν ἐρχομένοιο
Σκορπίου Ὠρίωνα περὶ χθονὸς ἔσχατα φεύγειν.

[32] S. Insler (1978 : 524) points to the particular significance of the summer section of the zodiac to Mithraism, yet one may doubt whether the monuments adduced support the suggestion. A season symbolized by the cult icon must stretch from Taurus to Scorpius; the heliacal setting of these constellations coincides indeed with the classical equinoxes in Aries and Libra,—but this is mere astrological speculation.

3. MITHRAS-ORION

Orion is the one constellation that closes the gap between Taurus and the other equatorial summer constellations. Mithras' identification with Orion thus becomes absolutely necessary if the constellations of the bull slaying scene are to be equatorial. But we are not reduced to inferences of this kind, however compelling, for there exists proof for Mithras being Orion in written sources.

Porphyry, the neo-Platonic philosopher of the later third century A.D., with his wide command of the Mithraic literature then available, constitutes one of our best literary sources for Roman Mithraism.[1] In his essay on the meaning of the cave in the Odyssey (13, 102-112) Porphyry reports, with approval, the views of the second-century Platonic and Pythagorean scholar Numenius :[2] the cave is an image and symbol of the cosmos of which the two extremities in the heavens are the tropic of Cancer and the tropic of Capricorn. These circles are assigned to the Moon and to Saturn respectively as the planets closest to and farthest from men. There follows a disquisition showing which signs of the Zodiac are the respective 'houses' of the seven planets,—obviously to further underpin the assignment of Cancer to the Moon as her 'house' and of Capricorn to Saturn as his 'house'.

After a description of Cancer and Capricorn as the northern gate for souls coming to genesis and the southern gate for souls leaving from genesis, Porphyry continues with an essential passage :[3]

---

[1] On Porphyry, Numenius, and his pupil Cronius and their reports about Roman Mithraism in general see R. Turcan (1975: 62ff.).

[2] Porphyrius-, *De Antro Nympharum* 21 ff. (= A. Nauck, 1886: 70ff.; Arethusa I, 1969: 22ff., with translation).

[3] Porphyrius, *De Antro Nympharum* 24 (= A. Nauck, 1886: 73; Arethusa I, 1969: 24): τῷ μὲν οὖν Μίθρᾳ οἰκείαν καθέδραν τὴν κατὰ τὰς ἰσημερίας ὑπέταξαν· διὸ κριοῦ μὲν φέρει Ἀρηίου ζῳδίου τὴν μάχαιραν, ἐποχεῖται δὲ ταύρῳ Ἀφροδίτης. ὡς καὶ ὁ ταῦρος δημιουργὸς δὲ ὢν ὁ Μίθρας καὶ γενέσεως δεσπότης κατὰ τὸν ἰσημερινὸν δὲ τέτακται κύκλον ἐν δεξιᾷ μὲν ἔχων τὰ βόρεια, ἐν ἀριστερᾷ δὲ τὰ νότια. This is the reading as given in A. Nauck's Teubner edition with the δέ after δημιουργὸς and the name of Mithras restored according to the manuscripts. As for punctuation, I placed a full stop after Ἀφροδίτης instead of a comma, and I removed the colon after δεσπότης.

'To Mithras they assigned his proper seat on the equinoxes
That is why he bears the sword of Aries, the sign of Mars, and
why he also straddles the bull of Venus. Like the bull a demiurge
and lord of genesis, he is placed on the equator, the north to his
right, the south to his left', ...

The sword Mithras is bearing, and the bull he is straddling, leave
no doubt that Mithras is seen here as the bull slayer of the cult icon.
But why do Aries and Taurus support his being on the equator?

The answer, we believe, is given by Aratus. In his famous description
of the equator, quoted above, he says of that circle: 'The sign for it
is the Ram and the knees of the Bull'.[4] It seems that Aries and Taurus
are adduced by Porphyry because they are the first two signs of the
equator and thereby support and explain Mithras' position on that
line. Disregard of Aratus' passage has led to different interpretations
of Porphyry's report. F. Cumont thought Taurus is mentioned here
because in remote 'Chaldaean' times the spring equinox was in
Taurus. Yet on the reckoning of the precession of the ecliptic, that
would lead us back at least to the third millennium B.C.—hardly a
convincing proposition, especially when considering the state of
Babylonian astronomy.[5]

Another suggestion was to emend the text of the manuscripts
radically so as to read '(Mithras) rides on the Bull of Venus; Libra
is the house of Venus as is the Bull'.[6] Thereby one would have gained
a reference, even though devious, to the second equinoctial point,
i.e. Libra, a reference that would well justify Mithras being on the
equinoxes. Unfortunately this latter solution is altogether invented and
has no support in the manuscript tradition. What both these proposed
solutions have in common is that they search for the *points* of the

---

[4] Aratus, *Phaenomena* 515 (= G. R. Mair, 246): σῆμα δέ οἱ Κριὸς Ταύροιό τε
γούνατα κεῖται. See also the scholia to Aratus 515 (= J. Martin, 1974:311): τὴν
κατάληψιν αὐτοῦ δίδωσιν ἐκ τῶν ἐπιψαυόντων αὐτῷ ζῳδίων. σημεῖον δὲ τοῦ κύκλου
ὁ Κριὸς ὁ πᾶς καὶ τὰ τοῦ Ταύρου γόνατα κεῖται.

[5] F. Cumont (1899: 201 but see *ibidem*, 210f.). The equinoxes are apparently a Greek,
not a Babylonian discovery, see D. R. Dicks (1966 and 1970). See also R. Beck (1977: 5f.).
A. Bouché-Leclercq (1899:134) figured the equinox was in Taurus from 4400 B.C.
to 2200 B.C.

[6] R. Beck (1976, b).

equinoxes while Porphyry actually is concerned with the *circle* of the equinoxes, i.e. the equator. Not only does he mention that circle expressly towards the end of the passage quoted, but he has it in mind also at the beginning of the passage in the phrase 'on the equinoxes', for Mithras is assigned only one seat and how could that be on both equinoctial points at the same time? Moreover, the context is the assignment of circles to the Moon and to Saturn so that one expects Mithras also to be given a circle, i.e. the equator.[7]

According to Porphyry, then, Mithras is on the Equator, and so is Orion. If Porphyry's passage hints at a responsibility of Mithras for the entire circle of the equator, the same can be parallelled, in Roman eyes, for Orion: Manilius, writing in the time of Augustus, proclaims of Orion:

'Under him as their leader the constellations orbit through all of the sky'.

This may mean either that Orion is the leader of all the constellations, or that he leads the equatorial constellations which wheel on the largest orbit and hence through all of the sky.[8] Elsewhere, too, Aratus and, following him, Cicero and Germanicus single out Orion, together with the equinoctial signs, as the significant constellation of the equator.[9]

---

[7] Elsewhere Porphyry uses the word κατά in the same way to designate the location of circles: ch. 21 the northern tropic is located κατά καρκίνον, the southern tropic κατ' αἰγόκερων. For a correct understanding of the passage discussed see R. L. Gordon (1975: 232) where Porphyry's word διό is seen in its proper function, i.e. the references to Aries and Taurus are made to support the statement that Mithras is on the circle of the equinoxes. Gordon (1976: 133) assumes perhaps rightly that Porphyry here refers to the layout of a Mithraic cave, but the symbolism cave = cosmos insures that the real cosmos is meant at the same time.

[8] M. Manilius, *Astronomicon* I, 395 (= A. E. Housman, 1937: 395): *hoc duce per totum decurrunt sidera mundum.* See Housman's excellent commentary, *ibidem.*

[9] Aratus, *Phaenomena* 231-232 (= G. R. Mair, 1921, 224): μεσσόθι δὲ τρίβει μέγαν οὐρανόν, ἧχί περ ἄκραι | χηλαὶ καὶ ζώνη περιτέλλεται Ὠρίωνος. Cicero, *Aratea* 230-231 (= V. Buescu, 1941: 191): (*Aries*) *nam caeli mediam partem terit, ut prius illae/Chelae, tum pectus qua cernitur Orionis*; Germanicus, *Aratus* 232-233 (= D. B. Gain, 1976: 28): (*Aries*) *terit hic medii divortia mundi,/ut Chelae, candens ut balteus Orionis.* According to Hyginus, *Astronomicon* 4, 3 (= B. Bunte, 1875, 102), Orion is girt by the equator itself: *ipso circulo praecinctus existimetur.*

Besides the fact that he is on the equator, we learn from Porphyry also that Mithras has the north to his right hand, the south to his left hand.[10] This completes the identification of Mithras as Orion, for of all the equatorial signs only Orion and Ophiuchus are in the shape of men and only Orion points with his right arm to the north and with his left arm to the south. Such at any rate is the way the ancient uranographers describe him. Aratus begins his portrayal of the constellations south of the zodiac with Orion, a fact explained by his scholiast as follows:[11] 'The poet began with Orion because he comes closest to the northern constellations; for while his belt is on the equator, he touches the zodiac with his right hand holding the club, and in his left he holds the starry skin'. In Roman times Orion is more often seen holding a sword in his right hand, but this weapon, too, points prominently to the north so that Ovid in his *Metamorphoses*, speaking of constellations pointing out north, could say:[12]

'... nor do I ask you to look for Bootes,
nor the Big Dipper, nor for the drawn sword of Orion'.

---

[10] R. Turcan (1975: 83f.) takes Porphyry's words not to mean the north and the south but the zodiacal signs in the northern hemisphere and the zodiacal signs in the southern hemisphere; however, Porphyry, in *De Antro* consistently uses τὰ βόρεια and τὰ νότια to designate the northern and the southern quarters of the heavens, never the signs of the Zodiac (see especially his chapter 29, with the contrasting terms τὰ ἀνατολικὰ and τὰ δυτικὰ; cf. Arethusa, 1969, *passim*).

[11] Scholia in Aratum vetera, 322 (= J. Martin, 1974: 239):
ἤρκται δὲ ὁ ποιητὴς ἀπὸ τούτου διότι συνεγγίζει μᾶλλον τοῖς βορείοις. γὰρ τὴν ζώνην κατὰ τὸν ἰσημερινόν, καὶ τῇ δεξιᾷ καλαύροπα κρατῶν ἐφάπτεται τοῦ ζῳδιακοῦ, ἐπὶ δὲ τῆς ἀριστερᾶς δορὰν ἔχει ἐνάστερον.

[12] Ovid, *Metamorphoses 9, 206f.*: *... nec te spectare Booten/aut Helicen iubeo, strictumque Orionis ensem.* Cf. Cicero, *Aratea* 587 (= V. Buescu, 1941: 243): *et dextra retinens non cassum luminis ensem.* For a Greek text of the Roman period see Valens (Boll, 1903: 68): νοτόθεν δὲ ὁ Ὠρίων ξίφος ἔχων ἐν τῇ δεξιᾷ χειρὶ ἀνατετακώς· τῇ εὐωνύμῳ κατέχει τὸ λεγόμενον κηρύκιον, ἐζωσμένος κατὰ μέσον τοῦ σώματος. The point here is that Orion in these Roman texts holds his sword in his upraised right hand. The sword hanging from Orion's belt is an old Greek view and is mentioned also by Aratus, *Phaenomena*, 587. In Germanicus' *Aratus*, 332 (= D. B. Gain, 1976: 31) that sword becomes a presumably empty *vagina ensis*, a mere sheath, because the hero holds the sword in his right. V. Buescu's (1941: 242, n. 5) comment on the text of Cicero wrongly assumes that the sword sheath below the belt is meant. See also the Scholia to Germanicus' *Aratus* (A. Breysig, 1867: 166, 15ff.): *habet autem stellas ... in gladio quem tenet in manu III.* Compare W. Gundel (1937: 985f.) for pictures.

Orion's widespread arms are also marked by Manilius :[13]

'Orion, stretching his arms over a great part of the heavens'.

Similarly, the only Roman representation of Orion as a hero shows him hunting in the netherworld, depicting him with his right arm characteristically raised and his left arm somewhat lowered (Fig. 5).[14]

Fig. 5. Orion hunting in the netherworld. From a wall painting of the Augustan period. Rome.

One may object that even if Porphyry sees Mithras as Orion with his right arm raised, Mithraic art does not, for on the bull slaying scenes Mithras' right arm is usually lowered, thrusting the sword into the animal's shoulder. Yet there is a notable series of bull slaying scenes that are exceptions to this rule. The Ostia statue by Kriton is the most well known of these : it shows Mithras, clad like a Greek hero with the Chiton rather than with the usual Persian trousers, as he raises his right arm with the sword to prepare for the fatal blow

[13] Manilius, *Astronomikon* I, 387-388 (= A. E. Housman, 1937: 39) : *cernere vicinum Geminis licet Oriona in magnam caeli tendentem bracchia partem.*
[14] Th. Kraus (1967, no. 117); F. Cumont (1945: 412ff.); M. F. Squarciapino (1962: 41); Küentzle (1902: 1023f.).

(Fig. 6).[15] A similar scene is found on a relief from Bulgaria with
Mithras in the nude like a Greek hero, also raising the sword high
in his right arm.[16]

Fig. 6. Statue of Mithras from Ostia.

This diverging iconographic pattern suggests that the knowledge
remained alive among Mithraists, as it did with Porphyry, that Mithras
was Orion, and hence he could be portrayed the way the Atlases and

---

[15] CIMRM 230 fig. 69, cf. fig. 248; Th. Kraus (1967, no. 268).

[16] CIMRM 2327. Not quite like this pattern but somewhat similar are two reliefs
one from Dacia and one from Rome, CIMRM 2196 and CIMRM 476-479 =
M. J. Vermaseren - C. C. van Essen (1965:130 and plates XIX and XX). These reliefs
show Mithras with his right arm held away from the bull and, characteristically for
their Greek inspiration, Mithras is nude except for a loincloth. On the highly unusual
relief CIMRM 1275 Mithras wears only a cape, but there, too, nudity combines with
the right hand away from the bull.

star maps showed him.[17] While on other monuments Mithras wears the Persian dress with the long trousers, on the monuments where he has his right arm raised he is nude or wearing the Greek Chiton which means he is purposely shown as a Greek hero, i.e. as Orion.

A major argument for the identification of Mithras with Orion comes from the Roman astral myth about Orion and Taurus. Just as the view of Orion with a drawn sword in his right hand is more characteristic of the Roman than of the Greek period, so is Orion's fight with the bull. Aratus' statement that Orion is located aslant beneath the bull is translated by Cicero thus:[18]

'Then Orion with bent body
Holds the lower part of the restive bull'.

Similarly, Vitruvius in his description of the heavens remarks that 'Orion, in oblique position, is near the hoof of the bull, holding it in his left, while raising the club with his other hand towards the twins'.[19] The Scholia to Germanicus say 'Orion stretches his hand towards the foot of Taurus'[20] and finally, Hyginus describes Orion thus:

---

[17] Or are these images simply following different Greek and Roman artistic models? Hardly, for its basic consistency suggests that the icon was designed only once for all times. For possible models see F. Saxl (1931:11ff.) and E. Will (1955:169ff.). E. Will (1978:530f.) suggests that our pattern (or at least the Ostia statue and the Santa Prisca relief (CIMRM 230 and 476-479) showing Mithras as Greek hero) are due to the fact that the meaning of the standard gesture of Mithras thrusting the sword into the bull's shoulder was no longer understood for what it meant originally, i.e. the killing of a defeated opponent. Yet there is clear evidence that this gesture of thrusting a sword into the shoulder of a defeated opponent was still understood in the second century A.D. by the Roman army and its artists, for one of the metopes of the Adamklissi monument shows just this act, see F. B. Florescu (1965:435, Metope 19, cf. p. 442, Metope 26).
[18] Aratus, *Phaenomena*, 322 (= G. R. Mair, 1921:232): Λοξὸς μὲν Ταύροιο τομῇ ὑποκέκλιται αὐτὸς Ὠρίων. Cicero, *Aratea* 322 (= V. Buescu, 1941:209): *Exinde Orion, obliquo corpore nitens, / inferiora tenet truculenti corpora Tauri.* Buescu's translation *'se tient sous les parties inférieures du farouche Taureau'* misrepresents the words *tenet corpora* as is proved by the passage of Vitruvius (see next note).
[19] Vitruvius 9, 5, 2 (= F. Granger, 1934:242): *Orion vero transversus est subiectus, pressus ungula tauri, manu laeva tenens (sc. eam), clavam altera ad geminos tollens.*
[20] *Scholia to Germanicus, Aratus* (E. Breysig, 1867:109, 6f.): *Ad tauri pedem protendit manum Orion.* The manuscript reading *manum* is preferable to Breysig's *manus* which would mean that Orion stretches both his hands towards the bull.

'fighting the bull, holding in his right hand the club and being girt with his sword, he is set towards the west'.[21]

The view was widely shared in Roman times that Orion was fighting Taurus. It follows that if the bull of the bull slaying scene is Taurus, then Mithras must be Orion. And it is obvious that the constellation Orion was eminently suited for this role, perceived as it was in the Roman period as the mighty hunter with his leaping dog, the sword in his right hand and grappling the bull with his left.[22]

Orion was not one of the twelve all-important constellations of the zodiac. How, then, could he assume this outstanding role in a cosmic religion? Orion had the great advantage of representing more accurately than any other constellation a man, i.e. a hero, or a god.[23] Orion, moreover is placed in the center of the heavens, girt by the equator itself,[24] besides, he is the largest of the constellations and the most brilliant of them all: his fires burn so brightly that 'night, mistaking him for day, folds her dark wings'.[25] In other words, he rivals the very sun.

If Mithras was Orion, why is he not named so in our sources? The reason may be that within the cult to call Mithras Orion would have meant to deprive the god of his true name, while outside the

---

[21] Hyginus, *Astronomica* 3, 33 (= B. Bunte, 1875: 95): *Hunc a zona et reliquo corpore aequinoctialis circulus dividit, cum Tauro decertantem collocatum, dextra manu clavam tenentem et incinctum ense spectantem ad occasum.* See ibidem 2, 33 (= 71): *negant tam nobilem et tam magnum venatorem de quo et ante in Scorpionis signo diximus, oportere fingi leporem venari.—Itaque Oriona cum Tauro decertantem fecerunt.*

[22] For Canis Minor as the dog of Orion see the following chapter.

[23] Aratus, *Phaenomena* 323ff. See also Germanicus, *Aratus* 329f. (= D. B. Gain, 1976: 31): '*Non ulla magis vicina notabit | stella virum, sparsae quam toto corpore flammae.*

[24] Hyginus, *Astronomica* 4, 3 (= B. Bunte, 1875: 102): *ipso circulo praecinctus existimetur.*

[25] Manilius, *Astronomicon* 5, 12 (= A. E. Housman, 1937, V, 2): *magni pars maxima caeli.* Ibidem 59f. (= 9): *quo fulgente super terras, caelumque trahente | ementita diem nigras nox contrahit alas.* Perhaps one may add that with Orion began, and ended, the calendar in the Metonic circle in Athens, see Aratus, *Phaenomena*, 752 (= G. R. Mair, 1921: 264, cf. p. 205), and that for Manilius, *Astronomicon* V, 58 (= A. E. Housman, 1937, vol. 5: 9) he is the mover of the heavens, *caelumque trahente*, which recalls the description of Mithras by Claudianus, *De consulatu Stilichonis* 1, 58ff. (= F. Cumont, 1896: 8) as *vaga… volventem sidera Mithram*, cf. F. Cumont (1899: 201).

cult there was a certain reluctance to reveal religious secrets.[26] Hence the knowledge that Mithras was Orion was shared by few but the Mithraists themselves.

---

[26] For the reluctance to reveal secrets of Mithraism in literature see the scholia to Statius, *Thebais* I, 717ff. (= F. Cumont, 1896:47): *His autem versibus sacrorum Solis mysteria patefecit.* There exists a faint possibility that the sixth-century chronographer Malalas preserves a mention of Orion in a Mithraic context when he says that Zarathustra, when about to die, 'invoked Orion and was taken away by fire from heaven' (J. Bidez - F. Cumont, 1938, vol. 2: 57B 51a: καὶ εὐξάμενος τὸν Ὠρίωνα ἀπὸ πυρὸς ἀερίου ἀνηλώθη). As the legendary founder of Mithraism one would expect Zarathustra to invoke Mithras rather than Orion, i.e. the two may be identified here. Yet the editors of the text have perhaps a more plausible explanation, i.e. that the myth of Orion was transferred to the hunter of the bible, Nimrud, (Genesis 10, 6ff.) and he in turn was identified with Zarathustra as the founder of Mesopotamian civilization. Still, since there is nowhere an explicit identification of Zarathustra with Orion, and since it is not easy to see how Zarathustra-Orion could have invoked himself, Malalas may here preserve the original identification of Mithras with Orion. Either way the story is of interest for the transfer of the myth of Orion to an Oriental figure.

4. THE IMAGE OF THE HEAVENS
AND THE CULT ICON

The bull slaying scene as a work of art derives its elements from the Greek and Roman image of the heavens. Indeed, some of these elements are portrayed with surprisingly close resemblance to the constellation pictures on the Atlas Farnese globe (Fig. 2). This is true in particular for Mithras himself. On the bull slaying scene he always reaches with his left knee and left arm towards the bull; frequently his upper body bends foreward, a sword hangs on his belt, and his head turns backwards—just as on the Atlas Farnese globe. A few icons, discussed above, show Mithras in the exact image of Orion with the raised right hand holding the sword, but possibly even the god's lowered right arm with the sword pointing downwards goes back to a variant view of Orion in the sky as a text of Hermes Trismegistos apparently suggests.[1]

Of the animals some details are also remarkable. The bull's left foreleg is consistently shown in the cult icon to be bent back,—in accordance with the Atlas Farnese globe and our written sources.[2] Similarly, the snake is always extended, never curled up. Of Canis Minor no ancient picture or detailed description survives but it is said to resemble closely Canis Maior which will mean that it was a dog leaping upwards as on the bull slaying scene.[3]

---

[1] See W. Gundel (1936: 197) placing the sword to where otherwise the fur or the shield of Orion is depicted.

[2] E. G. A. Bouché-Leclerq (1899: 134 fn. 3). Cicero, *Aratea* 330 (= V. Buescu, 1941: 239) *inflexoque genu proiecto corpore Taurus.*

[3] Eratosthenes, *Catasterismi* 42 (= K. Robert : 1878: 192, 14f.) : καὶ ποιεῖ ὁμοιότητα τοῦ Κυνός. Hyginus, *Astronomica* 3, 35 (= B. Bunte, 1875: 96) : *Procyon. Hic in lacteo circulo defixus, pedibus aequinoctialem circulum tangit. Spectat ad occasum.* The Carolingian miniature of the Leiden illustrated Aratus going back directly to a 4th century model shows Canis Minor leaping to the left, but the illustrations in this manuscript partly give the view from inside the sphere (Hydra) and partly from outside (Orion), so that nothing can be gained for the direction of the dog, except that it is leaping; see G. Thiele (1898: 130). Hermes Trismegistos (W. Gundel 1936: 58, 6) : *Anticanis cum radiis Canis erectus,* cf. ibid. 201 f.

As for the overall composition of the scene, the need for a well composed icon obviously necessitated some changes of the Greek image of the heavens. The most notable of these changes is the turning around of the bull and its representation as a complete animal rather than just the front portion of it, i.e. similar to the way it is represented on pictures of the Zodiac (see e.g. Frontispiece and Fig. 1). The other animals were grouped around Mithras and the bull. Dog, snake and scorpion kept their positions relative to each other but were moved underneath the main picture, while the raven was put further up. All figures, except for the bull and possibly Canis Minor kept their original orientation,—the great majority of the monuments even preserves the direction of the scorpion to the upper right with the sting curling to the upper left.[4]

Thus the changes from the image of the sky to the icon of the bull slaying scene are comparatively few and readily understandable as necessary for artistic reasons. No doubt, the turning around of the bull and its completion was needed in order to arrive at an icon following an accepted pattern of bull slaying, i.e. the model of Nike killing a bull as seen on the temple of Athena Nike on the Akropolis at Athens,[5] or that of Heracles fighting the Cretan bull.

The fact that all the elements of the bull slaying scene, and much of their iconography, are taken from the Greek image of the heavens is of the greatest importance not only for the origin but also for the meaning of the icon. In particular it precludes all primarily Iranian influence. No longer will one argue that the scorpion and the snake were added to the icon as the evil animals of Mazdaism, bent upon swallowing up the life-giving essences coming forth from the bull. Perhaps Mithras kills the bull in the image of the Iranian Ahriman or Saoshyant[6]—but if so, his deed was first assimilated to the exploit of

---

[4] When Crater is added it is generally to the right of the snake rather than on its back, and the lion, too, is to the right of the Crater rather than atop it : the connection between the signs is expressed instead by the snake curling up to the mouth of the Crater as if to drink from it (Frontispiece; Fig. 1) and by the lion frequently putting a paw on the Crater. In the Danubian examples, though, the lion is indeed atop the Crater, see CIMRM, vol. 2, plates figures 274 through 505.

[5] See F. Cumont (1899: 179f.); E. Will (1955: 169ff.).

[6] F. Cumont (1899: 186ff.). For the scorpion as the embodiment of evil see e.g. F. Saxl (1931: 67f.).

Orion in the sky. All the elements of the bull slaying scene are there because the Greeks saw them as the equatorial summer constellations. Any meaning they may have acquired in the context of Roman Mithraism is subsequent to this and hence secondary, possibly due more to artistic and fortuitous reasons than to theological ones. Thus, if an ear of corn had to be portrayed, the brushy end of the bull's tail, or the similar picture of blood on the bull's wound, may have invited one to place it there; and where else could the dog jump to more conveniently than to the bull's wound? Finally, the scorpion was placed at the bull's genitals because in Greek astrological tradition Scorpius ruled that part of the body.[7] It follows that Mithras' oriental dress on the icons is secondary, a fact corroborated by those icons discussed above that show the god in the dress of a Greek hero.[8]

Even features that have been explained theologically without reference to Mazdaism are now revealed as belonging to the Greek image of the heavens. Thus Mithras, while killing the bull, turns his head backwards not because he needs 'celestial inspiration' brought by the sun or by the raven, but primarily because Orion does so in the sky to watch the bear (Fig. 2).[9] Whether or not the Mithraists gave this feature a subsequent theological interpretation is not known. Certainly they did not need one originally.

---

[7] M. Manilius, *Astronomicon* II, 462 (= A. E. Housman, 1937:48): *et scorpios inguine gaudet.* Cf. F. Cumont (1899: 202), M. J. Vermaseren (1978: 33ff).

[8] Above, p. 23. For Mithras' *pileus* cap being Greek see F. Cumont (1899: 186ff.).

[9] 'Celestial inspiration': F. Cumont (1899: 193). Orion turns his head back on the Atlas Farnese globe (Fig. 2), obviously because Homer (Iliad 18, 488 = Odyssey 5, 274) says the bear is watching him and he, as a consequence, is looking back as described by Manilius, *Astronomicon* I, 502 (= A. E. Housman, 1937:49): *Arctos et Orion adversis frontibus ibant.* See also the scholia to Aratus 450 (= J. Martin, 1974: 283): καὶ γὰρ Ἄρκτος συνορᾶται καὶ <ἄλλα> θηρία παρ' αὐτῷ. Contra: F. Boll (1903: 166). For a good discussion of Mithras' facial expression see R. Turcan (1975: 144f.).

5. GREEK HERO

Mithras kills the bull because Orion does so. But who was Orion to the founders of Roman Mithraism? Certainly he was the hero embodied in the largest, most brilliant, even sun-like constellation of the sky. Yet besides this he was also the hero of Greek mythology. This raises the question of how far the myth of Mithras is the myth of Orion.

The myth of Orion as seen by Greek and Roman astronomers is told by Eratosthenes in these words:[1] 'When he came to Chios he got drunk and raped Merope, the daughter of Oinopion. Oinopion who could not stand this overbearing behaviour had him blinded and thrown out of the land. In his wanderings he came to Lemnos where he found Hephaistos who took pity on him and gave him his servant Kedalion whom he took as his guide, carrying him on his shoulders so he could point out the road. Going to the East and joining the sun he was healed, it seems, and thus went back to Oinopion to avenge himself. Oinopion, however, was hidden underground by his people. Despairing of finding him, Orion went to Crete to hunt with Artemis and Leto, apparently bragging he would kill all animals on earth. But Earth got angry at him and brought forth a huge scorpion that stung and killed him. At the request of Artemis and Leto, Zeus then put Orion among the stars because of his manhood—and likewise the animal to commemorate the deed'.

In other versions of the myth, Orion was a friend of Oinopion suing for the hand of Merope and as part of his suit cleared Chios of wild animals (or stole a lot of cattle as a bride's price for Merope), yet Oinopion made him drunk and blinded him in his sleep.[2]

Some of these mythological deeds of Orion were clearly taken over into the myth of Mithras. The most outstanding characteristic of Orion

---

[1] Erastosthenes, *Catasterismi* (Epitome) 32 (= K. Robert, 1878 : 162 f.). The most interesting passage reads: ἐλθὼν δ᾽ ἐπὶ τὰς ἀνατολὰς καὶ Ἡλίῳ συμμίξας δοκεῖ ὑγιασθῆναι. For collections of the myths about Orion see R. Graves (1955, vol. 1 : 151 ff.), Küentzle (1902), and especially Wehrli (1942).

[2] Apollodorus 1, 4, 3 (= J. G. Frazer, 1921 : 30 ff.); Aratus, *Phaenomena*, 637 ff. (= G. R. Mair, 1921 : 256). Cf. Wehrli (1942 : 1069, 35).

is his fame as a hunter; it is implied already by Homer in the Iliad
and in the Odyssey when he says that the bear is watching Orion.
Likewise, Mithras is prominently portrayed as a hunter, both in the
Orient and in Germany, and usually with bow and arrow, a weapon
carried also by Orion.[3] Orion's quarry included a great variety of
animals in the various forms of the myth, from the bear of Homer to
the hare of the constellation at his feet, and especially the bull, as
described above.[4] Mithras, too, hunts many different animals and it
may, or may not, have a special meaning that on one hunting scene
he is frontally opposed by the bull, just as is Orion in the sky.[5] If
Mithras is in any way related to Orion, his myth as a hunter must derive
from the hunter Orion, which suggests that other parts of the myth
of Mithras may also derive from the deeds of Orion.

The birth of Orion is related by Hyginus as follows :[6] 'Aristomachus

---

[3] CIMRM 52, 1137, 1247, 1292. Orion with the bow : Ὠρίωνα ὡς τοξότην. See
W. Gundel (1937: 986). For the bear watching Orion see above, page 30.

[4] Hyginus *Astronomica* II, 32 (= B. Bunte, 1875: 71): *Lepus. Hic dicitur Orionis
canem fugere venantis. Nam cum oportebat eum venatorem finxissent, voluerunt etiam
significare aliqua de causa; itaque leporem ad pedes eius fugientem finxerunt. Quem
nonnulli a Mercurio constitutum dixerunt, eique datum esse praeter cetera genera qua-
drupedum, ut alios pareret, alios habet in ventre. qui autem ab hac causa dissentiunt,
negant tam nobilem et tam magnam venatorem ... oportere fingi leporem venari .... Itaque
Oriona cum Tauro decertantem fecerunt.* See above, p. 25f.

[5] CIMRM 1137. There, too, he is followed by a leaping dog, just as Orion is
followed by Canis Minor, cf. Eratosthenes, *Catasterismi* 42 (= K. Robert, 1878: 192):
Ὠρίωνος δὲ κύων ἐστίν. Cf. the scholia to Aratus 450 (= J. Martin, 1974: 283):
Ὠρίωνος δὲ λέγεται Κύων, καὶ διὰ τὸ φιλοκύνηγον εἶναι ταῦτα αὐτῷ παρατεθῆναι
τὰ σημεῖα.

[6] Hyginus, *Astronomica* 2, 34 (= B. Bunte, 1875: 72): *Aristomachus autem dicit
quendam Hyriea fuisse Thebis, Pindarus autem in insula Chio. Hunc autem, cum Iovem
et Mercurium hospitio recepisset petisse ab his ut sibi aliquid liberorum nasceretur. Itaque
quo facilius petitum impetraret, bovem immolasse et his pro epulis adposuisse. Quod cum
fecisset, poposcisse Iovem et Mercurium quod corium de bove foret detractum et quod
fecerant urinae in corium infudisse, et id sub terra poni iussisse; ex quo postea natum
puerum, quem Hyrieus e facto Uriona appellaret, sed venustate et consuetudine factum
est, ut Orion vocaretur.* The story is also told by the scholia to Germanicus' *Aratus*
(B. Breysig, 1867: 63, 164, 166) with the three gods Iuppiter, Mercury, and Neptune;
similarly, Ovid, *Fasti* 5, 493ff. with fine commentary by F. Bömer (1958: 321f.) : οὐρέω
'to urinate' means here and elsewhere 'to pass sperm'. Of consequence are the lines
531f. *'omnes ad terga iuvenci constiterant—pudor est ulteriora loqui'* for they use the
same word for the bull in question as is used for the bull Mithras carries on his
shoulders (M. J. Vermaseren - C. C. van Essen, 1965: 200): *Hunc quem aur[ei]s humeris
portavit more iuvencum.* The story is also told by Servius' scholia on Vergil's *Aeneid*

says there was a certain Hyrieus ('Of the Beehives') at Thebes who asked Iuppiter and Mercury when they were his guests that a child be born to him. In order to have a better chance to get what he asked, he sacrificed a bull and offered it to the gods as their meal. Thereupon Iuppiter and Mercury told him to skin the bull, pour their urine on the hide, and bury it. Out of this a boy was born afterwards. Hyrieus called him Urion from what had happened, but because it sounded better he came to be called Orion'.

The similarity of this story to the myth of Mithras' birth is striking. Literary and epigraphic sources call Mithras 'rock-born', and on numerous reliefs and statues one sees the god as a boy emerging from the ground, holding a sword and a torch in his hands. (Fig. 7 and Frontispiece).[7]

Fig. 7. The Birth of Mithras. (After CIMRM 2184 and 2188).

I, 535 (= Servius, Harvard, 1946 : 240) with a suggestion that Mars rather than Neptune was in that company : *Oenopion rex cum filios non haberet a Iove, Neptuno, et Mercurio vel, ut quidam tradunt, non Neptuno sed Marte quos hospito susceperat, hortantibus petiit ut sibi filios darent.* etc. Mars was certainly brought in because Orion's most prominent attribute was his sword.

[7] F. Cumont (1899: 159ff.); despite his general favour for an Iranian origin of Roman Mithraism, Cumont does not think the myth of Mithras' rock birth is Iranian and hence suggests the cults of Asia Minor as its area of origin. For an Iranian origin of the birth myth see G. Widengren (1966: 444).

Our sources make it clear that 'rock born' (Mithras) and 'earth born'
(Orion) mean the same and could be used interchangeably;[8] hence
Mithras' miraculous birth is well-nigh identical with Orion's miraculous birth.[9] Since the birth myth is portrayed so frequently in
Mithraic art it must have been of central importance among the god's
deeds, second only to the bull slaying. Its meaning will be discussed
in the next chapter.

The prime myth Mithras shares with Orion is, of course, the fight
with the bull, for by Roman times, if not earlier, the bull had become
Orion's opponent in the sky.[10] True, astronomers still related the
stories of the scorpion as the killer of Orion, pointing to the fact that
when the scorpion rises, Orion sets in a never ending flight; but
understandably, Orion's defeats found little place in the myth of
Mithras and thus we hear nothing of his death by a scorpion nor of his
relations with women, except, possibly in the initiation grade of 'bride
groom' (nymphius). By contrast, Orion's successful deeds, even his
toils, were adopted and emphasized, particularly the myth of the fight
with the bull.[11]

Like Orion, Mithras is a cattle thief;[12] like him, he takes the bull

---

[8] Pseudo-Plutarch, *De Fluviis* 23, 4 (= F. Cumont, 1896, 36): Παράκειται δὲ αὐτῷ
ὄρος Διόρφον καλούμενον ἀπὸ Διόρφου τοῦ γηγενοῦς, περὶ οὗ φέρεται ἱστορία
τοιαύτη· Μίθρας υἱὸν ἔχειν βουλόμενος καὶ τὸ τῶν γυναικῶν γένος μισῶν πέτρᾳ τινὶ
προσεξέθορεν· ἔγκυος δὲ ὁ λίθος γενόμενος μετὰ τοὺς ὡρισμένους χρόνους ἀνέδωκε
νέον τοὔνομα Διόρφον. Even though this is a contrived story, the use of the word
γηγενής for someone born from the πέτρα is incontrovertible. Orion is called γηγενής
by Apollodorus 1, 4, 3 (= J. G. Frazer, 1921, 31) cf. Wehrli (1942: 1068).

[9] Possibly even the legend of the three gods and the bullhide was transferred to
Mithras, for the relief panel CIMRM 782 shows three men or gods at a banquet on
what may be a bullhide: the head of the bull is brought on a platter and the scene
is completed with the miraculous birth of Mithras. See also CIMRM 693, similarly
with a banquet of three. The concept of gods dining on a bullhide is familiar to
Mithraism as it is regularly found in the scenes of the banquet of Mithras and the
Sun god.

Perhaps G. Widengren (1966: 444) is right in that Hieronymus' words *in lapide vel
in terra de solo aestu libidinis ... generatos* (F. Cumont, 1896: 19) imply a possessor of
such libido, hence a father (or fathers) for Mithras.

[10] See above, p. 25f.

[11] For Mithras' toils see e.g. M. J. Vermaseren - C. C. van Essen (1965: 204).

[12] For Orion as cattle thief see Küentzle (1902: 1039); for Mithras see e.g. Porphyry,
De Antro Nympharum 18 (= A. Nauck, 1886: 69): βουκλόπος θεός, and the discussion
by R. Turcan (1975: 76f.).

by its legs.[13] A scene frequently portrayed on Mithraic reliefs and sculptures shows Mithras carrying the bull on his shoulders, or dragging the animal along, holding it by its legs.[14] A verse from the Mithraeum at Santa Prisca in Rome describes the deed thus :[15]

'This young bull which he was wont to carry on his golden shoulders'. The editors of the inscription did not comment on the word 'golden', but its meaning becomes clear from Vergil's description of Orion :[16]

'He watched Orion, armed with gold'.

Servius' scholion to Vergil's passage states that the gold in Orion's belt and sword refers to the brilliant star light they emit.[17] The same is of course true for the bright stars in Orion's shoulders, and thus the verse from the Santa Prisca Mithraeum is additional evidence for Mithras being seen as a heavenly body, i.e. the constellation Orion.

The fact that Mithras is Orion may perhaps explain still more of the myth about Mithras and the bull. Mithraic art depicts frequently scenes in which the god holds on to a runaway bull, or carries a bull, or drags a bull along. Could it be that Orion, when rising after Taurus, was seen as trying to hold on to the bull? Then, when wheeling underneath Taurus in mid-heaven, he was perhaps seen as carrying the bull, and finally, when setting before Taurus, he may have been seen dragging the bull.[18] No such myth survives of the Greek hero Orion, but such an interpretation of the myth of Mithras and the bull gains some support from the Mithraic expression for it, *transitus dei*, a phrase meaning the course of a heavenly body across the firmament.[19] If such was

---

[13] For Orion holding the bull by its legs see above, page 25, note 20.

[14] F. Cumont (1899: 171): not an Iranian idea.

[15] M. J. Vermaseren - C. C. van Essen (1965: 200ff.) : *Hunc quem aur[ei]s humeri[s p]ortavi[t] m[o]re i[u]vencum.*

[16] *Aeneid* 3, 517 : *armatumque auro circumspicit Oriona.*

[17] See the scholia to Vergil's passage in Servius (Harvard) (1965: 191) : '*armatum auro*' *quia et balteus et gladius clarissimis fingitur stellis.*

[18] For Orion's rise compared to Taurus see Hipparch, *Commentary* 3, 1, 9 (= K. Manitius, 1894: 226), for its setting *ibidem* 1, 7, 13-15 (= 70f.). For the comparable notion of Taurus 'carrying' the sun see e.g. Macrobius' *Commentarium in Somnium Scipionis* 1, 18, 15 (= J. Willis, 1970: 72, 23) : *Tauro gestante solem.*

[19] Cf. Macrobius, *Commentarii in Somnium Scipionis* 1, 20, 26 (= J. Willis, 1970: 83) : *cum transitu solis.* For the Mithraic expression see e.g. CIMRM 1494ff. and M. J. Vermaseren - C. C. van Essen (1965: 202). F. Cumont (1899: 171) thought of *transitus* as a passage over various obstacles.

indeed the myth of Mithras and the bull, it remains yet to be found whether it was made up by the founders of Roman Mithraism or adopted from a preexisting myth about Orion.

Both Orion and Mithras are solar heroes. The myth tells of Orion going to the Orient to join the sun god. There, Helios restores his eyesight. The Latin term for this, *lumina restituere*[20] means also 'to give light'. Since Orion's light is the light of the sun, he might be seen as a solar hero in one of his aspects, just like Mithras.[21] Modern mythographers, see in Orion a solar hero because, like the rising sun, he makes the wild animals disappear from the surface of the earth.[22] The myth that Orion went to the sun god to receive the light from him seems very well matched by the myth of Mithras going to the sun god and reaching for his crown of rays.[23] (Fig. 8).

Fig. 8. Mithras reaches for the sun god's crown of rays.

The other dealings of Mithras with the sun god are not known as deeds of Orion, but they could easily be imagined as such if Orion did not get the light without a fight and reconciliation. These deeds may be expressed in the myths of Helios kneeling before Mithras, Helios

---

[20] Scholia to Germanicus' *Aratea* (= A. Breysig, 1867: 163): *qui cum ad ortus solis venisset, a Sole dicuntur ei lumina restituta.*

[21] See the comparison of the sun's light with that of Orion by Hyginus, *Astronomica*, 4, 18 (= B. Bunte, 1875: 119) : *Solis stella nomine Phaeton, corpore est magno, colore autem igneo; similis eius stellae quae est in humero dextro Orionis.* Such a comparison may, or may not, have reinforced the myth. It must be stressed that neither Orion nor Mithras are identical with the sun god.

[22] R. Graves (1955: vol. 1, 153, n. 2); K. Kérenyi (1964: 186 ff.) subsumes Orion under 'Die Sonne, der Mond und ihre Sippe'.

[23] CIMRM 1083, 5. For the sun god as different from the light see the Roman medallion published by M. Guarducci (1959) with the inscription *Inventori lucis Soli invicto augusto.*

inviting Mithras onto his chariot, and Helios banqueting with Mithras over a bull's hide.[24] One may not give these possibilities more weight than mere speculations—which is what they are—, but the fact that both Orion and Mithras went to meet the sun god deserves serious consideration in a study of the origin and meaning of the myth of Mithras.

Perhaps yet another myth of Mithras has its origin in the deeds of Orion : the water miracle. According to the Greek and Roman view of the heavens, the river Eridanus or Oceanus springs from the left foot of Orion.[25] Admittedly, no myth survives, telling that Orion created this spring, and perhaps none existed; yet the origin of the sky river from Orion could well have given rise to the myth in which Mithras, by shooting an arrow at a rock, brought forth a spring.[26]

---

[24] For these myths see e.g. F. Cumont (1899: 172ff.). Two hypotheses might be added here, no more than speculations : 1) Orion's march to the Orient is described by one source as not under the guidance of Kedalion but on horseback. The scholia to Germanicus' Aratea (A. Breysig, 1867: 163, cf. K. Robert, 1878, 162) phrase it thus: *Vulcani auxilio usus dedit ei caballum qui eum ferret.* If this is an independent tradition, not a scribal error, then it would match those pictures where Mithras is shown riding on horseback without hunting, e.g. CIMRM 1289 and M. Duchesne-Guillemin (1978). Unfortunately, it is impossible to say whether on these monuments Mithras is blind or not. 2) A relief from Dieburg depicts the myth of Phaeton, CIMRM 1247, hence Mithraists concerned themselves with a change in the path of the sun. Could it be that the myth of Mithras and the Sun was about the sun's return to the equator? For the sun on the tropics see below, p. 42.

[25] See e.g. Vitruvius, *De architectura* 9, 5, 3 (= F. Granger, 1934, 242): *Profluit initium fontis capiens a laevo pede Orionis.* Cf. Eratosthenes, *Catasterismi* 37 (= K. Robert, 1878: 176): Οὗτος ἐκ τοῦ ποδὸς τοῦ Ὠρίωνος τοῦ ἀριστεροῦ τὴν ἀρχὴν ἔχει. Cf. W. Gundel (1937: 989ff.) and A. E. Housman (1937, vol. 1 : 44f.).

[26] For the Mithraic myth see e.g. F. Cumont (1899: 164ff.); also M. J. Vermaseren and C. C. van Essen (1965: 193) commenting on the line from Santa Prisca : *fons concluse petris qui geminos aluisti nectare fratres.* Perhaps there is a connection between the two rivers in the sky, joining each other, and the two twins, one for each hemisphere? At any rate, it seems that the river god or Oceanus reclining under the Santa Prisca bull slaying scene, represents Eridanus-Oceanus as seen in the sky under the left foot of Orion, cf. M. J. Vermaseren and C. C. van Essen (1965: 132 and plate XIX) (= CIMRM 476).

6. ROMAN GOD

Of all the Greek heroes Orion was by far the best suited to become a god of the Roman army during the empire. He was exceedingly strong and swift, as a soldier should be. He was armed, carrying a sword (*gladius*) and a baldric (*balteus*) which were so characteristic for him that he was commonly called 'the swordbearer'. Moreover, Orion wore the military belt (*cingulum*), the actual badge of Roman military service.[1] Orion was also the supreme master of that Roman military art, hunting. He was the epitome of manhood (*virtus*) for which he was put among the stars, he was a victorious army leader, the son of Mars, and the embodiment of a fierce warrior.[2] As a constellation he portended war by making the stars of his sword flare brightly—a sign of no mean importance to an army so much given to astrology as the Roman one.[3]

The fate of the individual soldier, too, was closely linked to Orion. According to a widespread popular belief the constellations imparted

---

[1] Strong: Homer, Iliad 18, 486 etc. see Wehrli (1942: 1081 f.) quoting Pindar, I.3-4, 67 Ὠαριωνεία φύσις. Swift: Aratus, *Phaenomena* 225-232, and especially Germanicus, *Aratus*, 332 (= D. B. Gain, 1976: 31): *pernici sic pede lucet*. See also the scholia to Aratus, *Phaenomena* 322 (= J. Martin, 1974: 238, 9 f.): σπουδὴν ἐνδεικνύμενος. Armed: Vergil, *Aeneid* 3, 517: *armatumque auro circumspicit Oriona*. Gladius: Servius' scholion to *Aeneid* 3, 517 (= Servius, Harvard, 1965: 191): *balteus eius et gladius clarissimis fingitur stellis*; scholia to Germanicus' *Aratus* (A. Breysig, 1867: 94, 6 f.): *aeternae balteus eius et gladius esse existimantur*; Germanicus, *Aratus* 3301 (= D. B. Gain, 1976: 31): *sic balteus ardet, sic vagina ensis*. Swordbearer: F. Boll (1903: 134), see also Ovid, *Fasti* 4, 388 (= F. Bömer, 1957: 196): *ensiger Orion*, etc. Cingulum: Hermes Trismegistos (W. Gundel, 1936: 55, 23): *oritur cingulum Orionis*, cf. Avienus, *Aratus*, 1375 (= Holder, 1887: 61, 50): *cingula ... Orionis*.

[2] For hunting as a *Romana militia* see Horace, Satires 2, 2, 10, cf. F. Cumont (1942: 438 ff.) *Virtus*: scholia to Germanicus' Aratus (A. Breysig, 1867: 164, 7): *ob virtutem* (a military term!), cf. Eratosthenes, *Catasterismi* 32 (= K. Robert, 1878: 164, 9): διὰ τὴν αὐτοῦ ἀνδρίαν. Warrior: Vergil, *Aeneid* 763 ff. Victorious leader of an army: Wehrli (1942: 1079).

[3] Portent of war: Lucanus, *Bellum Civile* 1, 665: *ensiferi nimium fulget latus Orionis*. Astrology in the imperial army: Tacitus, *Histories* 2, 78 reports how the select officers and soldiers of the Syrian and Judaean armies deliberate the proclamation of Vespasian *hortari, responsa vatum et siderum motus referre*; see also Cassius Dio 74, 14, 4; M. P. Nilsson (1974: 489).

their characteristics to those born under them, and thus Orion created officers and soldiers : huge, terrible, and powerful, marching through many lands, subduing barbarian nations.[4] To owe one's fate to Orion one need not be born just when he was rising on the eastern horizon, for astrological theory allowed constellations to be influential even when in mid-heaven, when setting, or anywhere else.[5]

Was Orion indeed worshipped by the Roman army or by Roman soldiers? A bronze statuette of a cow from near Damascus is the only evidence that has come to light. (Plate I).

Around its base, the monuments carries the following inscription :[6]

'Thamanaios the veteran piously set (me) up to the god Orion'.

The editor of the monument suggested Thamanaios dedicated the cow to Orion because he was fond of hunting. If so, would one not expect a wild animal rather than a cow? More likely, the cow denotes the constellation Taurus, seen by the Romans as the quarry of Orion. Taurus, whose hindquarters and sex are invisible in the sky, is frequently taken by astrologers to be a cow rather than a bull.[7] Whatever the cow may mean here —it could also represent a sacrificial animal— the essential point is that Thamanaios, a Roman veteran, worshipped Orion.

---

[4] Teukros (= F. Boll, 1903: 43) : Ὠρίων ξιφήρης στρατηγὸν, στρατηλάτην, στρα-τιώτην. Hermes Trismegistos (W. Gundel, 1936: 54, 12-17): *Quintus decimus gradus* (sc. *Tauri*) *cum fuerit horoscopus, in quo est stella splendida Orionis opposita stellae Antaris sitae in quinto decimo gradu Scorpionis, vocatur mors; facit tribunos, duces exercitus, militiae principes vel milites magnos et terribiles, impudicos vero et turpium perpetratores, potentes tamen per multam regionem peregrinantes et barbaras gentes subiugantes; violenta vero morte intereunt fraudulenter interfecti vel combusti.* The negative traits are also derived from the myth of the hero Orion, cf. W. Gundel (1936: 197 and *idem* 1937: 989).

[5] C. W. Gundel (1936: 141 and *idem*, 1949). Practically all constellations could be considered as 'paranatellonta', i.e. rising with a certain sign of the zodiac and thus influencing those born in it. Cf. A. Bouché-Leclercq (1899: 132 and 443). M. J. Vermaseren and C. C. van Essen (1965: 118) publish a Mithraic horoscope 'natus prima luce' for Nov. 20, A.D. 202—does it refer to Taurus and Orion setting in the morning sky?

[6] B. Zouhdi (1962). The inscription reads : Θαμαναῖος οὐετρανός εὐσεβῶν ἀνέθηκεν θεῷ Ὠρίωνι.

[7] Ovid, *Metamorphoses* 4, 717 : *vacca sit an taurus non est cognoscere promptum : pars prior apparet, posteriora latent.* Cf. A. Bouché-Leclercq (1899: 132ff.).

The Damascus cow with its inscription is of great importance in showing that Roman soldiers thought of Orion not as killed by the scorpion but alive, and a god to be worshipped. All the more surprising is the fact that this is the only dedication to Orion ever found in the entire Roman empire. Greek heroes enjoyed a considerable veneration in the imperial army: not only is Hercules honored in countless dedications but other heroes, too, are sometimes portrayed on engraved gemstones found in army camps.[8] Not so Orion— apparently the cult of Mithras had preempted the cult of Orion. Even the Damascus cow seems to belong to the first century A.D., i.e. before the rise of Mithraism.[9]

Beliefs about the constellation Orion also explain the social basis of Roman Mithraism. Since Mithras as Orion created the fate of soldiers and officers, he was worshipped above all by them. The only other noteworthy group of Mithraists were imperial and private slaves, especially civil servants such as tax collectors etc.[10] They must have adhered to the cult for the same reason as the soldiers, for according to Manilius Orion makes:[11]

'Smart souls, swift bodies, minds busy about their duty (*officium*), hearts attending all problems with speed and indefatigable vigor'.

Mithras-Orion, swiftest of all constellations (because the equator is the longest path around the sky),[12] creates the industrious civil servant

---

[8] See e.g. M. Henig (1970).

[9] B. Zouhdi (1962) dated the cow to the second century A.D., for stylistic reasons; yet it bears a strong resemblance to cows on coins of Augustus, e.g. BMC 659.

[10] C. M. Daniels (1975); R. L. Gordon (1973). F. Cumont's views (1899 and *idem*, 1923) that oriental soldiers and traders promoted the cult are not born out by the evidence as collected in CIMRM; E. Will (1978) overemphasizes the role of the merchants. R. L. Gordon (1973) rightly includes private slaves also as part of the god's constituency.

[11] M. Manilius, *Astronomicon* 5, 61-63 (= A. E. Housman, 1937, vol. 5:9):
sollertis animos, velocia corpora finget
atque agilem officio mentem curasque per omnis
indelassato properantia corda vigore.
On Manilius' naive method of collecting all the inferences from characteristics of the constellations, and extending his system to cover almost the entire heaven, see A. Bouché-Leclercq (1899: 132 and 443ff.).

[12] Aratus, *Phaenomena* 225-232.

Bronze statuette of a cow from Bloudan near Damascus, Syria. National Museum of Antiquities, Damascus.

Museum Photograph.

and slave as well as the soldier of unsparing effort by making them
go about their duties with speed and zest—the word *officium* is
characteristic for both. The essential fact that these two groups of
people were the main worshippers of Mithras has been noticed
before and rightly explained with the externalization and confirmation
by the cult of the values conducive to these stations in society.[13] Now
that we know Mithras-Orion as the creator and protagonist of soldiers
and (civil) servants, the exact nature of the relationship between the
god and his followers is revealed. Neither was it Iranian dualism
that fired Roman soldiers to become fighters of the light against the
darkness, nor was it the sun god's celestial invincibility that captured
the hearts of the soldiers and civil servants, but it was their relation
to the god who had made them what they were and who by his
example validated the virtues essential to their jobs.[14]

Finally, this relationship explains one of the most peculiar characteristics of Roman Mithraism, the absence of women. Since there
were no women soldiers nor women civil servants, or women
in leading functions in private slave operations, Mithras did not
create their fate or embody their virtues, hence they had no reason to
adhere to his cult.

Roman Mithraism, of course, was far more than a belief in the
astrological influence of the constellation Orion. Mithras was a god,
not just a hero or a constellation, and while the logical consequence
of astrology is atheism—the stars, not the gods, determine everything—

[13] R. L. Gordon (1973) with a fine description of these values.
[14] For doubts about F. Cumont's view of dualism, see e.g. R. L. Gordon (1975: 246f.);
doubts about the appeal of *invictus*: A. D. Nock (1937: 456), — even Isis was *invicta*
(CIL VI, 30747). One of the most remarkable aspects of the spread of Mithraism is
the establishment of a Mithraeum at Dura-Europos in A.D. 168, immediately after
this Mesopotamian fortress had changed hands from the Parthians to the Romans.
And that this was done by Palmyrenian troops whereas in Palmyra itself no Mithreum
has been found. I tried to explain the more Parthian traits of the Mithraism at Dura
by a conscious attempt to win over the Parthian god to the Roman side (M. P. Speidel,
1978), and I consider this still likely to be the case. I was wrong, however, to
contradict E. D. Francis (1975) who suggested that the Palmyrenian bowmen at Dura
thereby dedicated a shrine to the "god of the Roman soldier". Certainly, Mithraism
then was only beginning its spread and still far from being the most typical god of
the army, but in the sense discussed above, he was the "god of the Roman soldier"
from the beginning; correct: R. L. Gordon (1973: 111).

Mithras, with the inconsistency peculiar to all religion, was invoked by his adherents as their protector, retaining an ongoing interest in their lives as a true god would.

Our knowledge of Mithraic beliefs gains a great deal from the discovery of the equatorial emphasis in the bull slaying scene, for it supports an essential statement of Porphyry about Mithras. The god, Porphyry says, has his seat on the equator as a demiurge and lord of genesis. Souls coming from the Milky Way to genesis enter the cosmos-cave at the tropic of Cancer and leave it for immortality on the tropic of Capricorn.[15] One might be inclined to regard these statements as Porphyry's (or his sources') own Platonic-Pythagorean interpretation of Mithraism, not necessarily shared by the members of the cult.[16] However, the emphasis on the equator expressed in the bull slaying scene is evidence that Porphyry touched here on one of the essential beliefs of Roman Mithraism, for ever since Aratus a description of the equator, lying midway between and parallel to the tropics, entailed also a description of the two tropical circles as the basic and standard layout of the heavens, together with the zodiac.[17] (See above, fig. 4). This is also the image Porphyry presents. Hence Cautes and Cautopates, on either side of Mithras and in his exact likeness, only smaller, will signify the sun on the two tropical circles just as Mithras is the sun on the equator.[18] The bull slaying scene

[15] Porphyry, *De Antro Nympharum*, 21ff. (= A. Nauck, 1886: 70ff.; Arethusa 1, 1969: 22ff.). See above, p. 19. These were popular ideas, cf. J. Flamant (1977: 485ff.).

[16] For a full account of all the ramifications of these questions see R. Turcan (1975: passim).

[17] Aratus, Cicero, Germanicus, Manilius, Vitruvius, Hyginus, and the scholia to Aratus and Germanicus as discussed in chapter 2 and 3. The model is always Aratus, *Phaenomena* 460-558 (= G. R. Mair, 1921: 242-250).

[18] Inscriptions identify Cautes and Cautopates with Mithras the sun: CIMRM 639, 836, 1056, 1671. In the brilliant conjecture of the Arethusa-edition of Porphyry's *De antro Nympharum* (24) (Cf. R. Beck, 1976: 4 and note 10) Cautes is located to the south of the equator (i.e. on the tropic of Capricorn) standing for warmth and apogenesis, while Cautopates is located to the north of the equator (i.e. on the tropic of Cancer), standing for coldness, moisture, (CIMRM 694, cf. Porphyry l.c. 10) and genesis: τεταγμένου αὐτοῖς κατὰ μὲν τὸν νότον τῷ Καύτου διὰ τὸ εἶναι θερμὸν, κατὰ δὲ τὸν βορρᾶν τοῦ <Καυτοπάτου> διὰ τὸ ψυχρὸν τοῦ ἀνέμου. Porphyry's report is increasingly being acknowledged as correct and essential to Mithraic belief, cf. M. J. Vermaseren (1974: 28), R. L. Gordon (1976), and R. Beck (1977). Contra: F. Cumont (1899: 201). Moreover, Porphyry, l.c. 28 speaks of Cancer and Capricorn as the 'gates

thus portrays that universally admired Greek view of the heavens as the basis for the belief in the souls' journey through the gates of Cancer and Capricorn on the tropical circles.[19]

Another disputed attribute of Mithras may also find its explanation by the god's association with the equator. Since the celestial equator lies exactly in the middle of the world and since it is commonly described as the middle line, it becomes very likely that Mithras was indeed called 'the god of the middle' (μεσίτης) as he is named in a passage by Plutarch.[20] Yet he was not, as has been suggested, the god in the middle between light and darkness, between good and evil, or between god and mankind[21]—as the god on the equator he was the god of the middle part of the soul's journey, lord of genesis. This he will have been for all mankind, both according to Porphyry's account and in his role as sun god,[22] but he could still give particular attention to officers, soldiers, and civil servants of 'indefatigable vigor' whom he favoured because he was originally and essentially Orion the sword-bearer.

Our understanding of the Mithraic beliefs is enhanced also by the myth of the hero Orion, for the apparent identity of Orion's and Mithras' birth myth may explain the theological meaning of the bull slaying scene. Mithras-Orion is not only rock-born but also bull-born.

---

of the sun' ('Ηλίου πύλαι). For Cautes and Cautopates as aspects of the sun during certain parts of the year see F. Cumont (1899: 208 ff.), who also realized that the triple Mithras (τριπλάσιος Μίθρας) of Dionysios Areopagites (Ep. 7 = F. Cumont, 1896: 11) means the sun in three aspects, i.e. Mithras, Cautes, and Cautopates.

[19] Contra: R. Turcan (1975: 129 f.).

[20] Plutarch, De Iside 46 (= J. G. Griffiths, 1970: 190f., with commentary p. 474); see for recent discussions of the passage R. L. Gordon (1975: 228 ff.), and R. Turcan (1975: 14 ff.). Gordon is surely wrong in arguing (ibid. 232) that the equator is not in the middle of the universe: its middleness is emphasized by all authors—it may suffice to quote Manilius 1, 575 (= A. E. Housman, 1937, vol. 1: 54): in media mundi regione locatus. Mithras as the god of the middle has nothing to do with the planetary order, it seems, at least the Mithraic planetary order does not place the sun in the middle, see Gordon, l.c. 229 f., contra: R. L. Turcan (1975: 11 ff.).

[21] Between good and evil: Plutarch, De Iside 46, followed by F. Cumont (1899: 303, 306, 310); contra R. L. Gordon (1975: 228). Between god and mankind: F. Cumont (1923: 116).

[22] For the sun god see e.g. Macrobius, Saturnalia 1, 19, 17 (= J. Willis, 1970: 111): Sol auctor spiritus caloris ac luminis humanae vitae genitor et custos est et ideo nascentis δαίμων id est deus creditur.

He originated in a rotting bull hide, exactly how bees originate according to a widely held ancient belief told by Vergil at the conclusion of his *Georgics*. There the birth of bees from dead bulls becomes the symbol of rebirth and salvation of the Roman people under Augustus.[23] Porphyry, too, makes much of bees as the bull-born souls of the just coming to genesis, loudly buzzing; similarly in the netherworld scene of the Aeneid the souls of the great Romans coming to genesis also buzz like bees.[24] Now that the Orion myth suggests Mithras was hidden in a bullhide underground, one may find meaning in a much disputed passage by Porphyry :[25]

> 'Bull-born are bees, and souls going to genesis are bull-born, and a bull stealer is the god who heard genesis while he was hidden'.

The buzzing of the souls to be reincarnated being a major point in the myth,[26] Porphyry seems here to refer to what Mithras heard when he was hidden in the bull hide. This interpretation has the great advantage of keeping the reading of the manuscripts intact rather than substituting some imagined word chosen to fit a preconceived hypothesis. The case is parallel to Porphyry's passage on Mithras on the equator, where the readings of the manuscripts proved to be superior to any emendations.[27]

At any rate, bees were widely understood to have part in the divine soul, because they obey laws; also, bull-birth expresses the genesis

---

[23] Vergil, *Georgicon* 4, 281 ff. e.g. 284f. : *quoquo modo caesis iam saepe iuvencis insincerus apes tulerit cruor*. Remarkably, the same word *iuvencus* is used as in the Mithraea, see above, p. 32, note 6.

[24] Porphyry, *De Antro Nympharum* 15-19 (= A. Nauck, 1886 : 66-70; Arethusa 1, 1969 : 16-21). Vergil, *Aeneid* 6, 706 :

> *hunc circum innumerae gentes populique volabant*
> *ac velut in pratis ubi aestate serena*
> *floribus insidunt variis, et candida circum*
> *lilia funduntur : strepit omnis murmure campus.*

[25] Porphyry, *De Antro Nympharum* 18 (= A. Nauck, 1886 : 69; Arethusa 1, 1969 : 20) : βουγενεῖς δ' αἱ μέλισσαι, καὶ ψυχαὶ δ' εἰς γένεσιν ἰοῦσαι βουγενεῖς, καὶ βουκλόπος θεὸς ὁ τὴν γένεσιν λεληθότως ἀκούων. For the discussions see e.g. R. Turcan (1975 : 72 ff.).

[26] E. Norden (1927 : 306) : *Vergil ... gebraucht das Gleichnis, um das* τρίζειν *der Seelen zu versinnbildlichen.*

[27] Above, p. 20.

of the souls for a writer like Vergil.[28] It follows, not conclusively, but with a great likelihood, that Mithras, by slaying the bull, initiated the birth of the souls, especially the souls of the just, in the way of his own birth. Mithras' bull slaying thus is the act of creation, and Mithras is the creator.[29]

The bringing of souls to genesis is also salvation : it is so for the Romans in the bull-slaying, bee-creating myth of Aristaeus told by Vergil at the end of his *Georgics*, and it is so for the Mithraists according to a line preserved in the Mithraeum of Santa Prisca in Rome :[30]

'And us, too, you saved by spilling the eternal blood'.

---

[28] Vergil, *Georgicon* 4, 220 : *esse apibus partem divinae mentis.*

[29] See R. Turcan (1975 : 1). CIMRM 2006-2007 has the bull slaying scene with the inscription *IOS deo genitori r(upe) n(ato),*—whatever the correct expansion of IOS may be (*Invicto Orienti Soli?* etc.) the *genitor* must be Mithras because of the bull slaying scene. The *Iuppiter Sol Invictus* suggested by I. Tóth (1970) as different from Mithras is unparallelled and unconvincing because of the relief. R. Turcan (1975 : 78) states the Mithraic monuments and inscriptions do not show Mithras as the creator of the world but he does not discuss CIMRM 2006-2007 or 1676: *gen(itori) lum(inis).*

[30] M. J. Vermaseren and C. C. van Essen (1965: 217ff.) : *Et nos servasti eternali sanguine fuso.* Cf. R. Turcan (1975: 82).

7. CONCLUSION

If our argument has demonstrated 1) that the bull slaying scene represents the equatorial summer constellations from Taurus to Scorpius, 2) that the Mithras of the cult icon is the constellation Orion, and 3) that the myth of Orion (astral or heroic) gave rise, at least in part, to the myth of Mithras the bullslayer, the sun god, the rock-born, the hunter, and the creator of soldiers and officials, then the conclusion becomes inescapable that Mithraism is a Greek and Roman, not an Oriental religion. Mithraism thus constitutes above all a chapter in Greek mythology and in Roman religion, its closest parallel being the cult of Hercules in the Roman army.[1]

It follows that F. Cumont's assessment must be revised: the 'brilliant tissue of astrological allegories' did not hide, but reveal the mystical meaning of the sacred icon.[2] Mithraism is as Greek as the cosmology on which it is built, and if the Greek lands in Europe and Asia Minor have yet yielded few traces of the cult, this was not because of an innate Iranian-Greek antagonism but because few Roman soldiers were recruited and stationed in these lands.

If this was so, why was Mithraism in its own time thought to be a Persian cult? Why did a truly Greek religion present itself in Iranian garb? The founders of the cult must have shared the old Greek and Roman belief that the wisdom of the Orient was far superior to

---

[1] For the parallel with Hercules see A. D. Nock (1937:111); see also the perceptive concluding remarks of M. P. Nilsson (1974:675): 'Der Schluss ist unvermeidlich, dass die Mithrasmysterien eine einmalige Schöpfung eines unbekannten religiösen Genies sind, das auf der Grundlage gewisser, von ihm ausgewählter Mythen und Riten und unter Heranziehung von Elementen aus der damals verbreiteten Astrologie und aus griechischem Glauben eine Religionsform schuf, die sich fähig zeigte, einen Platz in der römischen Welt zu erobern. Eine Frage, die nicht mit Sicherheit zu entscheiden ist, bleibt ob die astrologischen Elemente aus der mit der babylonischen vermischten persischen Religion oder aus der am Ende der hellenistischen Zeit weit verbreiteten Astrologie übernommen sind'. The latter question can now be answered: the astrological elements are fully Greek. Similar results have been achieved in the field of art history: E. Will (1955) has shown that the cult icon is largely Greek and that it is mythological, depicting Mithras as a hero rather than as a god.

[2] F. Cumont (1899:203).

their own.[3] As for the majority of the followers, Tacitus' observation will have been valid, that foreign superstitions were on the increase,[4] a phenomenon that reached its climax in the Christian empire. Just as Greek wisdom now travelled under the names of the Magi so Greek religion seemed more authoritative under an Iranian semblance.[5]

The true act of founding Western Mithraism thus consisted in a transfer of the name, the trappings, and the prestige of Iranian Mithras to the cult of Orion in the Roman army as we know it from the Bloudan statuette. (Plate I).[6] Future finds may tell whether the Orion cult already before its change to Mithraism had acquired a cosmology emphasizing the celestial equator and the doctrine of the celestial migration of the souls. In either case, Mithraism was not an artificial religion but an orientalizing, and perhaps philosophizing, adaptation of an existing cult : the cult of Orion.

As a religion of the Roman army, Mithraism not only reflects the confidence of that army in the stars but evinces a highly developed religious life, providing, to be sure, a special place for the soldier, yet also establishing a comprehensive and detailed view of the cosmos and man's role in it, in this life and beyond.[7]

---

[3] For the Roman view that others could better trace the cosmos see Vergil, *Aeneid* 6, 847 ff. : *alii ... caelique meatus | describent radio et surgentia sidera dicent : | tu regere imperio populos, Romane, memento.*

[4] Tacitus, *Annals* 11, 15 : *externae superstitiones valescant.*

[5] J. Bidez and F. Cumont (1938 : passim). A closely comparable phenomenon are the famous 'Mysteries' ascribed to Mithras-Helios, cf. A. Dieterich (1923). Compare Nietzsche's '*Also sprach Zarathustra*'. See also R. Reizenstein (1927) 169 ff., and A. D. Nock (1937 : 455) : 'The tendency to value non-Greek wisdom as of fabulous antiquity was very strong'.

[6] M. P. Nilsson (1974 : 511) convincingly argues that above all the introduction of the solar calendar under Augustus made solar religion popular. This, too, points to an early imperial rather than a late Hellenistic date for the creation of Western Mithraism. Possibly the initiation of Nero into the cult of the Armenian Mithras gave an impetus. Pliny, *Nat. Hist.* 30, 17 (Tiridates of Armenia came to Nero) : *Magos secum adduxerat, magicis etiam cenis eum initiaverat.* Of course, the creation of the cult icon and the establishment of the seven grades were also essential.

[7] For the fact that the cults of the Roman army were by no means simplistic or confined to military purposes see my 'Iuppiter Dolichenus' (1978). For the religion of the Roman army in general see E. Birley (1978) and H. Ankersdorfer (1973). For the cosmic interest of mystery religions see S. Angus (1928 : 67 ff.).

ABBREVIATIONS

ANRW   *Aufstieg und Niedergang der römischen Welt. Geschichte und Kultur Roms im Spiegel der neueren Forschung. (Joseph Vogt gewidmet).* Ed. H. Temporini and W. Haase, Berlin-New York, 1972 ff.

BMC   British Museum Catalogue.

CIMRM   M. J. Vermaseren, *Corpus inscriptionum et monumentorum religionis Mithriacae.* 2 vols, Den Haag, 1956 and 1960.

RE   Pauly-Wissowa, *Realencyclopädie der classischen Altertumswissenschaft*, Leipzig 1890 ff.

BIBLIOGRAPHY

Angus, S., *The Mystery Religions. A Study in the Religious Background of Early Christianity.* London, 1928.

Ankersdorfer, H., *Studien zur Religion des römischen Heeres von Augustus bis Diokletian.* Diss. Konstanz, 1973.

Barbulescu, M., *Cultul lui Hercules in Dacia Romana. Acta Musei Napocensis* 14, 1977, 173-194, and 15, 1978, 219-233.

Beck, R., *Interpreting the Ponza Zodiac. Journal of Mithraic Studies* 1, 1976, 1-19.

Beck, R., *The Seat of Mithras at the Equinoxes : Porphyry, De Antro Nympharum 24. Journal of Mithraic Studies* 1, 1976, 95-98.

Beck, R., *Cautes and Cautopates : Some Astronomical Considerations. Journal of Mithraic Studies* 2, 1977, 1-17.

Betz, H. D., *The Mithras Inscriptions of Santa Prisca and the New Testament. Novum Testamentum* 10, 1968, 62-80.

Bidez, J., - Cumont, F., *Les Mages hellénisés. Zoroastre, Ostanes et Hystaspe d'après la tradition grecque.* 2 vols. Paris, 1938.

Birley, E., *The Religion of the Roman Army : 1895-1977.* ANRW II/16.2, 1978, 1506-1541.

Boll, F., *Sphaera. Neue griechische Texte und Untersuchungen zur Geschichte der Sternbilder.* Leipzig, 1903.

Bömer, F., *P. Ovidius Naso, Die Fasten. Herausgegeben, übersetzt und kommentiert.* 2 vols. Heidelberg, 1957-58.

Borbein, H., *Der Kampf mit dem Stier. Römische Mitteilungen, Ergänzungsheft* 14, 1968.

Bouché-Leclercq, A., *L'astrologie grecque.* Paris, 1899.

Breysig, A., *Germanici Caesaris Aratea cum Scholiis.* Berlin, 1867. Reprint Hildesheim, 1967.

Buescu, V., *Ciceron, Les Aratea. Texte établi, traduit et commenté.* Bucharest, 1941. Reprint Hildesheim, 1966.

Buffière, F., *Les mythes d'Homère et la pensée grecque.* Paris, 1956.

Bunte, B., *Hygini Astronomica. Ex codicibus a se primum collatis.* Leipzig, 1875.

Campbell, L. A., *Mithraic Iconography and Ideology.* Leiden, 1968. (= EPRO 11).

Cumont, F., *Textes et monuments figurés relatifs aux mystères de Mithra. Vol. 2: Textes et monuments*. Brussels, 1896.

Cumont, F., *Textes et monuments figurés relatifs aux mystères de Mithra. Vol. 1: Introduction*. Brussels, 1899.

Cumont, F., *Oriental Religions in Roman Paganism*. New York, 1911. (Authorized translation from the French).

Cumont, F., *Astrology and Religion among the Greeks and Romans*. London, 1912.

Cumont, F., *Die Mysterien des Mithra. Ein Beitrag zur Religionsgeschichte der römischen Kaiserzeit*. Ed. K. Latte. Leipzig, 1923.

Cumont, F., *Recherches sur le symbolisme funéraire des Romains*. Paris, 1942.

Cumont, F., *Rapport sur une mission à Rome. CRAI* 1945, 386-420.

Daniels, C. M., *The Role of the Roman Army in the Spread and Practice of Mithraism*. In : J. R. Hinnells (1975), 249-274.

Dicks, D. R., *Solstices, Equinoxes and the Presocratics. Journal of Hellenic Studies* 86, 1966, 26-40.

Dicks, D. R., *Early Greek Astronomy to Aristotle*, London, 1970.

Diels, H., - Kranz, W., *Die Fragmente der Vorsokratiker*. 7th ed. Berlin, 1954.

Dieterich, A., *Eine Mithrasliturgie*. 3rd ed. by O. Weinreich, Leipzig, 1923.

Duchesne-Guillemin, M., *Une statuette equestre de Mithra. Acta Iranica* 17, 1978, 201-204.

Flamant, J., *Macrobe et le Néo-Platonisme latin, à la fin du VIe siècle*. Leiden, 1977.

Florescu, F. B., *Das Siegesdenkmal von Adamklissi*. Bucharest-Bonn, 1965.

Frazer, J. G., *Apollodorus*. 2 vols. London, 1921.

Gain, D. B., *The Aratus ascribed to Germanicus Caesar*. London, 1976.

Gordon, R. L., *Mithraism and Roman Society: Social Factors in the Explanation of Religious Change in the Roman Empire. Journal of Religion and Religions*, 1973, 92-121.

Gordon, R. L., *Franz Cumont and the Doctrines of Mithraism*. In : J. R. Hinnels (1975), 215-248.

Gordon, R. L., *The Sacred Geography of a Mithraeum: the Example of Sette Sfere. Journal of Mithraic Studies* 1, 1976, 119-165.

Granger, F., *Vitruvius on Architecture*. Edited from the Harleian Manuscript 2767 and translated into English, vol. 2. London, 1934. (LCL).

Graves, R., *The Greek Myths*, 2 vols. Baltimore, Maryland, 1955.

Griffiths, J. G., *Plutarch's De Iside et Osiride*; edited with an introduction, translation and commentary. Cardiff, 1970.

Guarducci, M., *Sol Invictus Augustus. Rendiconti della pontifica accademia Romana d'archeologia* 30-31, 1959, 161-169.

Gundel, H. G., *Zodiakos. Der Tierkreis in der antiken Literatur und Kunst*. München, 1972. (Offprint from Pauly-Wissowa, *Realencyclopädie der classischen Altertumswissenschaft*, vol. X, A).

Gundel, W., *Neue astrologische Texte des Hermes Trismegistos. Funde und Forschungen auf dem Gebiet der antiken Astronomie und Astrologie*. München, 1936. (= Sb. Bayer. Akad. Wiss., Phil.-Hist. Abt. NF 12).

Gundel, W., *Sternbilder, Sternglaube und Sternsymbolik bei Griechen und Römern*. In : Roscher, *Mythologisches Lexicon*, vol. 6, 1937, 869-1071.

Gundel, W., *Paranatellonta*. RE 8/2, 1949, 1214-1275.

Heath, T., *Aristarchus of Samos, The Ancient Copernicus. A History of Greek Astronomy to Aristarchus*. Oxford, 1913.

Henig, M., *The Veneration of Heroes in the Roman Army. The Evidence of Engraved Gemstones. Britannia* 1, 1970, 249-265.

Hinnels, J. R., (ed.), *Mithraic Studies. Proceedings of the First International Congress of Mithraic Studies*. 2 vols. Manchester, 1975.

Hinnels, J. R., *Reflections on the Bull-Slaying Scene*. In : J. R. Hinnels (1975), 290-312.

Holder, A., *Rufi Festi Avieni Carmina*. Innsbruck, 1887.

Housman, A. E., *M. Manilii Astronomicon*. 2nd ed. Cambridge, 1937.

Insler, S., *A New Interpretation of the Bull-Slaying Motif*. In : *Hommages à Maarten J. Vermaseren*, ed. M. B. de Boer and T. A. Edridge, vol. 2, Leiden, 1978, 519-538.

Kerényi, K., *Die Mythologie der Griechen*. 3rd ed. Darmstadt, 1964.

Kraus, Th., *Das römische Weltreich*. Berlin, 1967. (= *Propyläen Kunstgeschichte*, vol. 2).

Küentzle, *Orion*. In : Roscher, *Mythologisches Lexikon*, vol. 3, 1, 1902, 1018-1047.

Maas, E., *Commentariorum in Aratum reliquiae.* Berlin, 1898.

Mair, G. R., *Aratus.* Cambridge, Mass., 1969. (= Loeb C. L. 129).

Manitius, K., *Hipparchi in Arati et Eudoxi Phaenomena commentariorum libri tres.* Leipzig (Teubner), 1894.

Manitius, K., - Neugebauer, O., *Ptolemäus, Handbuch der Astronomie, Band II. Deutsche Übersetzung und erläuternde Anmerkungen von K. Manitius. Vorwort und Berichtigungen von O. Neugebauer.* Leipzig, 1963.

Merkelbach, R., *Die Kosmogonie der Mithrasmysterien. Eranos-Jahrbuch 1965 (Form als Aufgabe des Geistes).* Zürich, 1966, 219-257.

Nauck, A., *Porphyrii Philosophi Platonici Opuscula Selecta.* 2nd ed. Leipzig, 1886.

Nilsson, M. P., *Geschichte der griechischen Religion*, vol. 2, *Die hellenistische und die römische Zeit.* 3rd ed. Munich, 1974.

Nock, A. D., *The Genius of Mithraism. The Journal of Roman Studies* 27, 1937, 108-13. (= A. D. Nock, 1972, 452-458).

Nock, A. D., Review of CIMRM I. In : *Gnomon* 30, 1958, 291-295.

Nock, A. D., *Posidonius. The Journal of Roman Studies* 49, 1959, 1-15. (= A. D. Nock, 1972, 853-876).

Nock, A. D., *Essays in Religion and the Ancient World* (ed. Z. Steward). 2 vols. Cambridge, Mass., 1972.

Norden, E., *P. Vergilius Maro, Aeneis Buch VI.* Leipzig, 1927.

Oikonomides, A. N., *Mithraic Art. A Search for Unpublished and Unidentified Monuments.* Chicago, 1975.

Reizenstein, R., *Die hellenistischen Mysterienreligionen nach ihren Grundgedanken und Wirkungen*, 3rd ed., 1927 (Reprint Darmstadt, 1966).

Ristow, G., *Mithras im römischen Köln.* Leiden, 1974 (= EPRO 42).

Robbins, F. E., *Ptolemy, Tetrabyblos.* London, 1940.

Robert, K., *Eratosthenis Catasterismorum Reliquiae.* Berlin, 1878.

Robert, L., *Monnaies grecques de l'époque impériale. Revue Numismatique* 18, 1976, 25-56.

Saxl, F., *Mithras.* Leipzig, 1931.

Servius (Harvard), *Servianorum in Vergilii Carmina Commentariorum editio Harvardiana*, vol. 2, 1946; vol. 3, 1965.

Speidel, M. P., *Parthia and the Mithraism of the Roman Army.* In : *Acta Iranica (Encyclopédie permanente des études iraniennes)* 17, 1978, 479-483.

Speidel, M. P., *The Religion of Iuppiter Dolichenus in the Roman Army*. Leiden, 1978. (= EPRO 63).

Squarciapino, M. F., *I culti orientali ad Ostia*. Leiden, 1962. (= EPRO 13).

Stark, K. B., *Die Mithrassteine von Dormagen. Nebst anderen Ineditis des Mithrasdienstes. Jahrbuch des Vereins für Altertumsfreunde im Rheinlande* (= *Bonner Jahrbücher*) 46, 1868, 1-22.

Thiele, G., *Antike Himmelsbilder. Mit Forschungen aus Hipparchos, Aratos und seinen Fortsetzern und Beiträgen zur Kunstgeschichte des Sternhimmels*. Berlin, 1898.

Tóth, I., *The Cult of Iuppiter Sol Invictus Deus Genitor in Dacia. Acta Classica* (Debrecen) 6, 1970, 71-74.

Turcan, R., *Mithras Platonicus. Recherches sur l'héllénisation philosophique de Mithra*. Leiden, 1975. (= EPRO 47).

Vermaseren, M. J. - van Essen, C. C., *The Excavations in the Mithraeum of the Church of Santa Prisca in Rome*. Leiden, 1965.

Vermaseren, M. J., *Mithriaca I. The Mithraeum at S. Maria Capua Vetere*. Leiden, 1971. (= EPRO 16).

Vermaseren, M. J., *Mithriaca II. The Mithraeum at Ponza*. Leiden, 1974. (= EPRO 16).

Vermaseren, M. J., *Mithriaca IV*. Leiden, 1978. (= EPRO 16).

Wehrli, *Orion. RE* 18, 1942, 1065-1082.

Widengren, G., *The Mithraic Mysteries in the Greco-Roman World with Special Regard to their Iranian Background*. In : *La Persia e il mondo greco-romano. Accademia Nazionale dei Lincei, Quaderno no. 76*. Rome, 1966, 433-455.

Wikander, S., *Études sur les mystères de Mithras. Yearbook of the New Society of Letters at Lund*, 1950, 3-46.

Will, E., *Le relief cultuel gréco-romain. Contribution à l'histoire de l'art de l'empire romain*. Paris, 1955.

Will, E., *Origine et nature du Mithriacisme. Acta Iranica* 17, 1978, 527-536.

Willis, I., *Ambrosii Theodosii Macrobii, Commentarii in Somnium Scipionis*. Leipzig, 1970.

Willis, I., *Ambrosii Theodosii Macrobii Saturnalia*. Leipzig, 1970.

Zouhdi, B., *The Legend of Orion and the Statuette from Bloudan* (In Arabic), *Annales Archéologiques Arabes Syriennes* 11-12, 1961-1962, 89-98.

INDEX